Grades 7–12

# Algebra Problems

## One Step Beyond

**Reuben  Schadler**

**DALE SEYMOUR PUBLICATIONS**

This book is printed on recycled paper.

Illustrations: Bill Eral
Cover art: Julie Peterson

ISBN  0-86651-545-3
Order number DS21104

**DALE
SEYMOUR
PUBLICATIONS**
P.O. BOX 10888
PALO ALTO, CA 94303          7 8 9 10-MA-99

# CONTENTS

Problems designed to be solved with the use of a calculator are indicated by (C) following the problem.

# PREFACE

No classroom problem-solving effort is possible without good problems. Good problems often can't be created in the midst of a classroom situation. It takes time and planning to create problems that allow for different solution strategies, that can be varied and extended, that provide a good chance for success, that have understandable math, and that ask students to apply what they know to new situations. Unlike geometry, where good problems are hard to find, algebra lends itself to a plethora of problems, some of which I have included in this book.

With this book I have tried to give a collection of problems that supplement a first-year algebra course. I have tried to cover all the major topics in the course. The fact that most of my students seem to have a difficult time with problems involving distance, rate, and time may account for the number of problems that include this concept. As the book progresses, however, use of this formula requires more advanced algebra skills.

Solving problems isn't always easy; sometimes it is hard work. But if you as a teacher are enthusiastic about solving problems, students tend to solve problems with more enthusiasm. Although there *are* right answers to the problems in this book, there are *no* exactly right approaches to solving the problems. We can show students that the pleasure in reaching a successful solution generally makes the effort worthwhile.

R.S.

# INTRODUCTION

*Algebra Problems: One Step Beyond* is a collection of 33 sets of problems for students in grades 7 through 12 or for students who are currently studying algebra. Each set contains four related problems, labeled A, B, C, and D. Problem A is a warm-up problem that eases students into the work of Problem B, the main problem. Problem C is an extension problem that takes the students into more difficult but related concepts, and Problem D is a follow-up for later use to reinforce the concept.

## About the Book

Each of the 132 problems—warm-ups, main problems, extensions, and follow-up problems—appears in this book on a separate reproducible worksheet page, with ample space allowed for students to work out their solutions. In addition, Problems A, B, and C— the warm-up, main, and extension problems—also appear on a single page for teachers who wish to provide students with a choice of problems to solve. You may duplicate the pages and distribute them as in-class assignments, homework, math club activities, or extra-credit assignments.

Answers and solutions are found at the end of each problem set. For some problems, answers may vary, but at least one set of answers is provided.

## Using the Problems

The problem sets are arranged to follow the standard ninth-grade algebra curriculum, starting with order of operations and concluding with various uses of quadratics. There is no required order for using the 33 sets of problems, however; simply choose those sets that best suit your students' learning situation.

These problems are not the sort that your students will necessarily solve using the concept intended, but since there is more than one way to come up with solutions, individual approaches are encouraged. Showing the students the more "elegant" way increases their interest and shows them the power of the concepts they are learning.

You may find the chart on page ix a helpful tool for reminding your students of steps they should follow when they attempt a problem. You may wish to give a copy to each student. A poster form of the chart is available from Dale Seymour Publications.

# A GUIDE TO PROBLEM SOLVING

| | |
|---|---|
| To understand a problem, try these suggestions. | • Read the problem carefully.<br>• Decide what you're looking for.<br>• Find the important information. |
| To develop your plan, use some of these ideas. | • Guess and check.<br>• Draw a picture.<br>• Look for a pattern.<br>• Make a model.<br>• Act it out.<br>• Use easier numbers.<br>• Write a number sentence.<br>• Make an organized list.<br>• Make a table or chart.<br>• Use logic.<br>• Work backwards. |
| To check your work, follow these steps. | • Make sure you used *all* the important information.<br>• Check any arithmetic you may have done.<br>• Decide if your answer makes sense.<br>• Write your answer in a complete sentence. |

This chart is adapted from *Teaching Problem Solving: What, Why and How* by Randall Charles and Frank Lester, © 1982, Dale Seymour Publications.

## Problem Set 1
## ORDER OF OPERATIONS

### A. Groups Make the Difference

Insert parentheses, if needed, in each of the following expressions so that all have the same value.

$4 + 3 \cdot 7 - 4$       $2 \cdot 5 - \dfrac{1}{2} \cdot 10 \cdot 9$

$2 \cdot 3 + 3 \cdot 5$       $3^2 \div \dfrac{1}{3} + 3 \cdot 6$

### B. Where's My Substitute?

Given the following formulas:

$$Q = \pi ad ; \qquad m = \sqrt{d^2 - a^2} ; \qquad P = \frac{1}{3}\pi a^2 m$$

If $Q = 2310$, $\pi = \dfrac{22}{7}$, and $a = 21$, find the value of $P$.

### C. Does the Fork Go on the Left or Right?

Using *only* the symbols +, −, x, and ÷ as replacements for the blanks, find the greatest value of the expression given.

$1 \_ 2 \_ 3 \_ 4 \_ 5 \_ 6 \_ 7 \_ 8$

What would be the greatest value if you could also use parentheses?

### 1-A GROUPS MAKE THE DIFFERENCE

Insert parentheses, if needed, in each of the following expressions so that all have the same value.

$4 + 3 \cdot 7 - 4$

$2 \cdot 3 + 3 \cdot 5$

$2 \cdot 5 - \dfrac{1}{2} \cdot 10 \cdot 9$

$3^2 \div \dfrac{1}{3} + 3 \cdot 6$

### 1-B WHERE'S MY SUBSTITUTE?

Given the following formulas:

$$Q = \pi ad ; \qquad m = \sqrt{d^2 - a^2} ; \qquad P = \frac{1}{3} \pi a^2 m$$

If $Q = 2310$, $\pi = \dfrac{22}{7}$, and $a = 21$, find the value of $P$.

## 1-C    DOES THE FORK GO ON THE LEFT OR RIGHT?

Using *only* the symbols +, −, x, and ÷ as replacements for the blanks, find the greatest value of the expression given.

1 __ 2 __ 3 __ 4 __ 5 __ 6 __ 7 __ 8

What would be the greatest value if you could also use parentheses?

## 1-D    BUT DOES MY DEAR AUNT SALLY CARE?

Using all five of the following numbers and
any of the usual arithmetic operations,
parentheses, or exponents, show how you can
obtain the desired results. (You must use all
five of the numbers exactly once, and
exponents can take the place of one or more
of the blanks.)

2, 4, 9, 14, 17

____ ____ ____ ____ ____ = 1

____ ____ ____ ____ ____ = 2

____ ____ ____ ____ ____ = 3

## Problem Set 1
## ANSWERS AND SOLUTIONS

### A. Groups Make the Difference

**Answer:** 45

**Solution:**
Each expression will equal 45 when the parentheses are inserted as follows:

$(4 + 3)7 - 4 = 45$ $(2 \cdot 5 - \frac{1}{2} \cdot 10)9 = 45$

$(2 \cdot 3 + 3)5 = 45$ $3^2 + \frac{1}{3} + 3 \cdot 6 = 45$

### B. Where's My Substitute?

**Answer:** $P = 12{,}936$

**Solution:**
To find the value of $P$, first find the values of $d$ and $m$. Using $Q = \pi a d$ implies

$$d = \frac{Q}{\pi \cdot a} = \frac{2310}{\frac{22}{7} \cdot 21} = \frac{2310}{22 \cdot 3} = \frac{2310}{66} = 35$$

Using $m = \sqrt{d^2 - a^2}$,

$$m = \sqrt{35^2 - 21^2} = \sqrt{1225 - 441} = \sqrt{784} = 28$$

$$P = \frac{1}{2} \cdot \frac{22}{7} \cdot 21 \cdot 21 \cdot 28$$
$$= 12{,}936$$

### C. Does the Fork Go on the Left or Right?

**Answer:** 40,321

**Solution:**
Continued multiplication usually produces the greatest product, so think of $1 \cdot 2 \cdot 3 \cdot 4 \cdot 5 \cdot 6 \cdot 7 \cdot 8$. But using a + between the 1 and 2 results in a product that is 1 greater. Therefore, $1 + 2 \cdot 3 \cdot 4 \cdot 5 \cdot 6 \cdot 7 \cdot 8$ is the greatest product. The greatest product if parentheses may be used is 60,480. $(1+ 2) \cdot 3 \cdot 4 \cdot 5 \cdot 6 \cdot 7 \cdot 8$ produces this result.

### D. But Does My Dear Aunt Sally Care?

**Answer:** See Solution.

**Solution:**
This problem is patterned after a math game called Krypto. Many different solutions are possible, and the elegance of the solution depends on operations allowed—that is, powers and square roots or just +, −, x, ÷ with parentheses. The following solutions use only +, −, x, ÷, or parentheses.

$(\underline{9} + \underline{14}) \div (\underline{2} + \underline{4} + \underline{17}) = 1$
$(\underline{17} - \underline{14}) - (\underline{9} - \underline{2} \cdot \underline{4}) = 2$
$\underline{4} \cdot \underline{9} - \underline{14} - \underline{17} - \underline{2} = 3$

## Problem Set 2
## EQUATION SOLVING

### A. Gauss or Grouse? Any Takers?

Find the difference between the sum of the first 100 positive multiples of three and the sum of the first 100 positive even integers.

### B. This Smells Like Work!

The local fish market is having a sale on whole fish. The prices are as follows:

- You can buy an albacore and a barracuda for $21.
- You can buy a barracuda and a carp for $24.
- You can buy a carp and a dogfish for $32.
- You can buy a dogfish and an eel for $37.
- You can buy an eel and a flounder for $31.
- You can buy a flounder and a gar for $25.
- You can buy a gar and an albacore for $26.

Determine the cost of each individual fish.

### C. Just Carve, Please!

Suppose five pumpkins are weighed two at a time in all possible ways. The weights in pounds are recorded as 16, 18, 19, 20, 21, 22, 23, 24, 26, and 27. How much does each individual pumpkin weigh? (No fractions, please.)

## 2-A GAUSS OR GROUSE? ANY TAKERS?

Find the difference between the sum of the first 100 positive multiples of three and the sum of the first 100 positive even integers.

### 2-B  THIS SMELLS LIKE WORK!

The local fish market is having a sale on whole fish. The prices are as follows:

- You can buy an albacore and a barracuda for $21.
- You can buy a barracuda and a carp for $24.
- You can buy a carp and a dogfish for $32.
- You can buy a dogfish and an eel for $37.
- You can buy an eel and a flounder for $31.
- You can buy a flounder and a gar for $25.
- You can buy a gar and an albacore for $26.

Determine the cost of each individual fish.

## 2-C  JUST CARVE, PLEASE!

Suppose five pumpkins are weighed two at a time in all possible ways. The weights in pounds are recorded as 16, 18, 19, 20, 21, 22, 23, 24, 26, and 27. How much does each individual pumpkin weigh? (No fractions, please.)

### 2-D  THREE'S A CROWD!

Instead of the pumpkins being weighed two at a time, as in a previous problem, they are weighed three at a time, with the weights in pounds recorded as 27, 28, 30, 31, 32, 33, 35, 36, and 38. With this information, find the weight of the middle pumpkin. (*Hint:* Let $a$, $b$, $c$, $d$, and $e$ represent the weight of the pumpkins, with $a < b < c < d < e$. Find $c$.)

# Problem Set 2
## ANSWERS AND SOLUTIONS

### A. Gauss or Grouse? Any Takers?

**Answer:** 5050

**Solution:**

A knowledge of Gauss' formula for adding consecutive integers is valuable for an elegant solution to this problem.

The formula for finding the sum $1 + 2 + 3 + \cdots + n$ is $\dfrac{n(n+1)}{2}$.

$(3 + 6 + 9 + \cdots + 300) - (2 + 4 + 6 + \cdots + 200)$ can be written as $3(1 + 2 + 3 + \cdots + 100) - 2(1 + 2 + 3 + \cdots + 100)$, or simply $1 + 2 + 3 + \cdots + 100$. This sum is 5050.

$$\frac{100(1 + 100)}{2} = \frac{100(101)}{2} = 50(101) = 5050$$

### B. This Smells Like Work!

**Answer:** Using $a$ for albacore, $b$ for barracuda, $c$ for carp, etc., $a = \$12$, $b = \$9$, $c = \$15$, $d = \$17$, $e = \$20$, $f = \$11$, and $g = \$14$.

**Solution:**

Although this problem can be solved by using a system of equations, a more elementary solution involving only a substitution technique is possible. Using letters instead of words, the following equations can be formed: $a + b = 21$, $b + c = 24$, $c + d = 32$, $d + e = 37$, $e + f = 31$, $f + g = 25$, and $g + a = 26$. Adding the left and right sides of these equations results in

$$2a + 2b + 2c + 2d + 2e + 2f + 2g = 196$$
or
$$a + b + c + d + e + f + g = 98$$

Substituting the values $a + b = 21$, $c + d = 32$, and $e + f = 31$ leads to a solution.

### C. Just Carve, Please!

**Answer:** 7 lb, 9 lb, 11 lb, 12 lb, 15 lb

**Solution:**

If we let the weights of the pumpkins be $a$, $b$, $c$, $d$, and $e$ with $a < b < c < d < e$, then

| | | | |
|---|---|---|---|
| $a + b$ | $b + c$ | $c + d$ | $d + e$ |
| $a + c$ | $b + d$ | $c + e$ | |
| $a + d$ | $b + e$ | | |
| $a + e$ | | | |

represent all the possible weights.

This problem is impossible to do with a system of equations because it is not possible from the data given to tell which pairs equal which weighings. It is possible, however, to know the lightest, next lightest, next heaviest, and heaviest pairs. Since $a < b < c < d < e$, $a + b$ is the lightest, $a + c$ is the next lightest, $d + e$ is the heaviest, and $c + e$ is the next heaviest. Using the same technique as used in 2-B, adding all the variable combinations and all the number possibilities results in the equation

$$4a + 4b + 4c + 4d + 4e = 216$$
or
$$a + b + c + d + e = 54$$

Since $a + b$ is the lightest pair and $d + e$ is the heaviest pair, $a + b = 16$ and $d + e = 27$, resulting in $16 + c + 27 = 5$, or $c = 11$. Backtracking, since $a + c$ is the next lightest, $a + c = 18$, and $a = 7$; $a + b = 16$, and $b = 9$. $c + e$ is the next heaviest, so that $c + e = 26$, and $e = 15$, $d + c = 27$, and $d = 12$.

### D. Three's a Crowd!

**Answer:** 11 lb

**Solution:**

Weighing 5 things 3 at a time results in 10 possibilities. Consider $a < b < c < d < e$. Then

| | | |
|---|---|---|
| $a + b + c$ | $b + c + d$ | $c + d + e$ |
| $a + b + d$ | $b + c + e$ | |
| $a + b + e$ | $b + d + e$ | |
| $a + c + d$ | | |
| $a + c + e$ | | |
| $a + d + e$ | | |

are the possible weights.

Again, it is impossible to assign each of the 10 weights to a specific combination, but assignment of weights is possible for some of the combinations. For example, $a + b + c = 27$, $a + b + d = 28$, $c + d + e = 38$, and $b + d + e = 36$.

Combining each variable combination and each weight results in

$$6a + 6b + 6c + 6d + 6e = 324$$
or
$$a + b + c + d + e = 54$$

Since $a + b + c = 27$, $27 + d + e = 54$ and $d + e = 27$. Then, since $c + d + e = 38$,

$$c + 27 = 38$$
$$c = 11$$

Incidentally, the respective weights are 7, 9, 11, 12, and 15 lb.

### Problem Set 3
### PERCENTS WITH EQUATIONS

#### A. How About Breakfast?

Joel is taking his friend Jo Ellen to lunch. He has exactly $15 to spend and plans to leave a 15% tip. What is the maximum-priced lunch he can buy?

#### B. Can't We Just Count the Votes?

In a recent student body election, Adam received 40 more than 40% of the votes. Brigitte received 40 less than 50% of the number Adam received. Carl received 20 more than 50% of what Brigitte received, and Diane received the remaining 180 votes. How many votes were cast in the election and who was the winner?

#### C. What's the Bottom Line?

A purchase is made under the following conditions. There is a 25% discount because of a sale, a 10% discount because of the size of the order, and a 5% discount for not using a credit card. The discounts are taken successively. If a customer pays $1385.10, which includes an 8% sales tax, what was the original purchase price before tax and any of the discounts? (Successively means taken one at a time, not together.)

### 3-A HOW ABOUT BREAKFAST?

Joel is taking his friend Jo Ellen to lunch. He has exactly $15 to spend and plans to leave a 15% tip. What is the maximum-priced lunch he can buy?

### 3-B CAN'T WE JUST COUNT THE VOTES?

In a recent student body election, Adam received 40 more than 40% of the votes. Brigitte received 40 less than 50% of the number Adam received. Carl received 20 more than 50% of what Brigitte received, and Diane received the remaining 180 votes. How many votes were cast in the election and who was the winner?

### 3-C  WHAT'S THE BOTTOM LINE?

A purchase is made under the following conditions. There is a 25% discount because of a sale, a 10% discount because of the size of the order, and a 5% discount for not using a credit card. The discounts are taken successively. If a customer pays $1385.10, which includes an 8% sales tax, what was the original purchase price before tax and any of the discounts? (Successively means taken one at a time, not together.)

### 3-D  BUT DID THEY GIVE GREEN STAMPS?

Amir was offered a radio by one firm at
$80—less a discount of 20%, followed by
a 10% discount. Another firm offered him
the same radio at $80—less a 30% discount.
Which is the better offer and by how much?

## Problem Set 3
## ANSWERS AND SOLUTIONS

### A. How About Breakfast?

**Answer:** $13.04

**Solution:**
If $x$ represents the cost of the meal and $0.15x$ represents the amount of the tip, the equation $x + 0.15x = 15.00$ will give the solution.

### B. Can't We Just Count the Votes?

**Answer:** 700 votes; Adam won with 320 votes.

**Solution:**
If $x$ represents the total number of votes, then

$$0.4x + 40 = \text{votes for Adam}$$
$$0.5(.4x + 40) - 40 = \text{votes for Brigitte}$$
$$0.5[0.5(0.4x + 40) - 40] + 20 = \text{votes for Carl}$$
$$180 = \text{votes for Diane}$$
$$0.4x + 40 + 0.5(0.4x + 40) - 40 + 0.5[0.5(0.4x + 40) - 40]$$
$$+ 20 + 180 = x$$
$$0.7x + 210 = 0.3x$$
$$700 = x$$

### C. What's the Bottom Line?

**Answer:** $2000

**Solution:**
If $x$ represents the original price, $0.75x$ is the price after the 25% discount, $0.9(0.75x)$ is the price after the 10% discount, $0.95[0.9(0.75x)]$ is the price after the 5% discount, and $1.08\{0.95[0.9(0.75x)]\}$ is the price after 8% sales tax is added.

$$1.08\{0.95[0.9(0.75x)]\} = 1385.10$$
$$0.69255x = 1385.10$$
$$x = 2000$$

### D. But Did They Give Green Stamps?

**Answer:** The second firm's 30% discount is the better offer by $1.60.

**Solution:**
The first firm will charge $0.9[0.8(80)]$, or $57.60, whereas the second firm will charge $0.7(80)$, or $56.

### Problem Set 4
### PYTHAGOREAN POSSIBILITIES

### A. Why Not Elevens?

It is possible to have a right triangle with sides that are consecutive multiples of 7. Find it if you can and explain how you found it.

### B. Some Numbers Aren't Square!

How many of the numbers from 1 to 100 can be written as the sum of the squares of two positive integers? How did you find your answer?

### C. Integer Squares Leave Nothing Left Over

Show how the numbers 458, 685, and 1690 can be written as the sum of two integral squares.

## 4-A WHY NOT ELEVENS?

It is possible to have a right triangle with sides that are consecutive multiples of 7. Find it if you can and explain how you found it.

### 4-B SOME NUMBERS AREN'T SQUARE!

How many of the numbers from 1 to 100 can be written as the sum of the squares of two positive integers? How did you find your answer?

### 4-C INTEGER SQUARES LEAVE NOTHING LEFT OVER

Show how the numbers 458, 685, and 1690
can be written as the sum of two integral
squares.

## 4-D  CLOSE COUNTS ONLY IN  HORSESHOES!

Using only a compass and a straightedge, demonstrate how to locate *exactly* the point on the given number line that is associated with the irrational number $\sqrt{52}$.

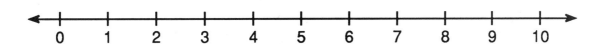

# Problem Set 4
## ANSWERS AND SOLUTIONS

### A. Why Not Elevens?

**Answer:** 21, 28, 35

**Solution:**

This problem can be solved at this point by using trial and error and the fact that the numbers 3, 4, and 5 are a Pythagorean triple.

### B. Some Numbers Aren't Square

**Answer:** 35

**Solution:**

$1^2 + 1^2 = 2$    $2^2 + 2^2 = 8$    $3^2 + 3^2 = 18$    $4^2 + 4^2 = 32$

$2^2 + 1^2 = 5$    $3^2 + 2^2 = 13$    $4^2 + 3^2 = 25$    $5^2 + 4^2 = 41$

$3^2 + 1^2 = 10$    $4^2 + 2^2 = 20$    $5^2 + 3^2 = 34$    $6^2 + 4^2 = 52$

$4^2 + 1^2 = 17$    $5^2 + 2^2 = 29$    $6^2 + 3^2 = 45$    ~~$7^2 + 4^2 = 65$~~

$5^2 + 1^2 = 26$    $6^2 + 2^2 = 40$    $7^2 + 3^2 = 5$    $8^2 + 4^2 = 80$

$6^2 + 1^2 = 37$    $7^2 + 2^2 = 53$    $8^2 + 3^2 = 73$    $9^2 + 4^2 = 97$

$7^2 + 1^2 = 50$    $8^2 + 2^2 = 68$    $9^2 + 3^2 = 90$

$8^2 + 1^2 = 65$    $9^2 + 2^2 = 85$

$9^2 + 1^2 = 82$

**9**      **8**      **7**      **5**

~~$5^2 + 5^2 = 50$~~    $6^2 + 6^2 = 72$    $7^2 + 7^2 = 98$

$6^2 + 5^2 = 61$    ~~$7^2 + 6^2 = 85$~~

$7^2 + 5^2 = 74$    $8^2 + 6^2 = 100$

$8^2 + 5^2 = 89$

**3**      **2**      **1**

### C. Integer Squares Leave Nothing Left Over

**Answer:** See Solution.

**Solution:**

$458 = 13^2 + 17^2 = 169 + 289$

$685 = 18^2 + 19^2 = 324 + 361$

$1690 = 13^2 + 39^2 = 169 + 1521$

### D. Close Counts Only in Horseshoes

**Answer:** See Solution.

**Solution:**

To locate $\sqrt{52}$, try to find two perfect squares whose sum is 52. Since $16 + 36 = 52$, a right triangle with legs of 4 and 6 will have a hypotenuse of $\sqrt{52}$. Using $\sqrt{52}$ as the radius, draw an arc to intersect the number line at $\sqrt{52}$.

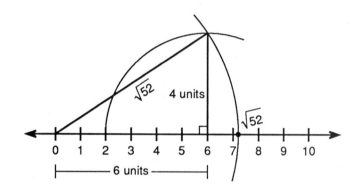

### Problem Set 5
### RATIONAL NUMBER ODDITIES

### A. Why No Repeat?

What rational number, when you write it as a decimal, starts out 0.115384615?

### B. Repeat Offenders

Given that $13^2 = 169$, $133^2 = \underline{17},\underline{689}$, $1333^2 = \underline{1},\underline{776},\underline{889}$, and $13,333^2 = \underline{177},\underline{768},\underline{889}$, examine the pattern and try to find two other numbers less than 20 that display this same type of number pattern. Illustrate your answer.

### C. Lady Macbeth Special

Exactly $57.245\overline{724}$% of the people who were asked if they used BLEM-OUT face cream replied yes. What is the *fewest* number of people who could have been asked the question?

## 5-A WHY NO REPEAT?

What rational number, when you write it as a decimal, starts out 0.115384615?

## 5-B REPEAT OFFENDERS

Given that $13^2 = 169$, $133^2 = \underline{17{,}6}8\underline{9}$, $1333^2 = \underline{1}{,}77\underline{6}{,}88\underline{9}$, and $13{,}333^2 = \underline{1}77{,}7\underline{6}8{,}88\underline{9}$, examine the pattern and try to find two other numbers less than 20 that display this same type of number pattern. Illustrate your answer.

## 5-C LADY MACBETH SPECIAL

Exactly 57.245724% of the people who were asked if they used BLEM-OUT face cream replied yes. What is the *fewest* number of people who could have been asked the question?

## 5-D TRY, TRY AGAIN

Place the numbers one through nine in the following arrangement to make three equal fractions.

$$\frac{\bigcirc}{\bigcirc} = \frac{\bigcirc}{\bigcirc \; \bigcirc} = \frac{\bigcirc \; \bigcirc}{\bigcirc \; \bigcirc}$$

## Problem Set 5
## ANSWERS AND SOLUTIONS

### A. Why No Repeat?

**Answer:** $\dfrac{3}{26}$

**Solution:**

Using a calculator is the best way to solve this problem. Let $A = 0.115384615$. Since $A \approx \dfrac{1}{9}$, try values that are close to $\dfrac{1}{9}, \dfrac{2}{18}, \dfrac{3}{27}$, and so on.

### B. Repeat Offenders

**Answer:** 16 and 19

**Solution:**

$16^2 = 256$

$166^2 = 27{,}556$

$1666^2 = 2{,}775{,}556$

$16{,}666^2 = 277{,}755{,}556$

$19^2 = 361$

$199^2 = 39{,}601$

$1999^2 = 3{,}996{,}001$

$19{,}999^2 = 399{,}960{,}001$

### C. Lady Macbeth Special

**Answer:** 1111 people

**Solution:**

The goal is to change $0.\overline{5724}$ into a fraction expressed in lowest terms. The denominator of the fraction will represent the number of people asked. If $n = 0.\overline{5724}$ and $10{,}000n = 5724.\overline{5724}$,

$9999n = 5724$

$$n = \frac{5724}{9999} = \frac{1908}{3333} = \frac{636}{1111}$$

### D. Try, Try Again

**Answer:** $\dfrac{3}{6} = \dfrac{9}{18} = \dfrac{27}{54}$

**Solution:**

Each fraction is equal to $\dfrac{1}{2}$. Putting the numbers 1 through 9 on slips of paper and rearranging them is one of the best solution techniques.

## Problem Set 6
## LEVER PRINCIPLE

### A. It All Comes Out Equal

If you are given a lever 12 ft in length and want to balance with someone weighing 200 lb, find the distance *you* would have to sit from the center (fulcrum). What value are you using for your weight?

### B. Double Trouble

Examine the diagram.

Two objects on each side of a lever can balance if $M_2d_2 + M_1d_1 = M_3d_3 + M_4d_4$. The four animals on the following balance weigh a total of 41 lb. If the kitten weighs 3 lb and the dog weighs 23 lb, find the weight of the rabbit and the raccoon so that the seesaw balances.

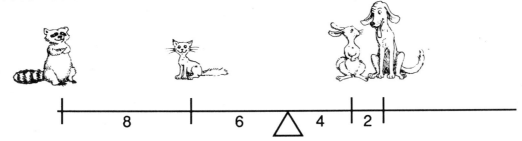

### C. Don't Leave 'Em Hanging!

Use the principle of the lever to find each of the missing weights that will enable the mobile to balance.

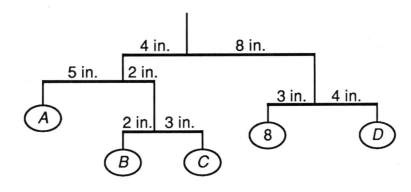

## 6-A  IT ALL COMES OUT EQUAL

If you are given a lever 12 ft in length and want to balance with someone weighing 200 lb, find the distance *you* would have to sit from the center (fulcrum). What value are you using for your weight?

## 6-B  DOUBLE TROUBLE

Examine the diagram.

Two objects on each side of a lever can balance if $M_2 d_2 + M_1 d_1 = M_3 d_3 + M_4 d_4$. The four animals on the following balance weigh a total of 41 lb. If the kitten weighs 3 lb and the dog weighs 23 lb, find the weight of the rabbit and the raccoon so that the seesaw balances.

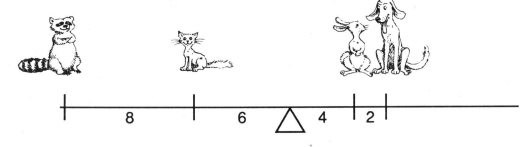

### 6-C  DON'T LEAVE 'EM HANGING!

Use the principle of the lever to find each of the missing weights that will enable the mobile to balance.

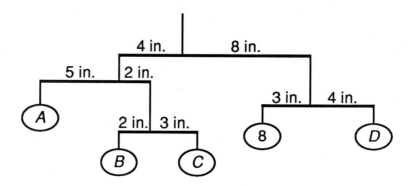

© Dale Seymour Publications

## 6-D  YOU MUST START SOMEWHERE!

The meter stick shown is balanced at the 50-cm mark. Notches on the meter stick, at multiples of five, indicate places where weights can be placed. Given four weights of 2, 3, 4, and 5 kg, show where they can be placed on the meter stick, two on each side of the balance point, to keep the balance (two weights cannot be placed on the same mark).

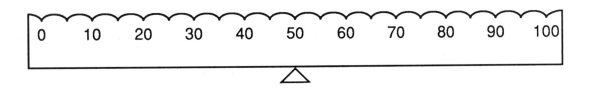

# Problem Set 6
## ANSWERS AND SOLUTIONS

### A. It All Comes Out Equal

**Answer:** Answers vary. See Solution.

**Solution:**

This is a basic lever problem. $x \cdot y = 200(12 - y)$. Solving for $y$ gives $y = \dfrac{2400}{200 + x}$. Thus if you weigh 100 lb, $y = 8$, so you would have to sit 8 ft from the center.

### B. Double Trouble

**Answer:** The rabbit weighs 5 lb; the raccoon, 10 lb.

**Solution:**

The combined weight of the raccoon and rabbit is 15 lb. Let $x$ = weight of rabbit. Then $15 - x$ = weight of raccoon.

$$3 \cdot 6 + (15 - x)14 = 4 \cdot x + 6 \cdot 23$$
$$18 + 210 - 14x = 4x + 138$$
$$90 = 18x$$
$$5 = x$$

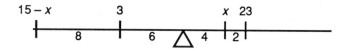

### C. Don't Leave 'Em Hanging!

**Answer:** $A = 8$, $B = 12$, $C = 8$, $D = 6$

**Solution:**

Looking at the mobile, the easiest weight to find is $D$, since $8 \cdot 3 = 4 \cdot D$. Therefore, $D = 6$. The combined weight on the right of the mobile is 14, resulting in a force of $8 \cdot 14$, or 112, on the right. To balance, there must also be a force of 112 on the left. The combined weights of of $A$, $B$, and $C$ must be 28, since $4 \cdot 28 = 112$.

$$5 \cdot A = 2(28 - A) \qquad B + C = 20 \qquad\qquad C = 8$$
$$5A = 56 - 2A \qquad\quad 2B = 3(20 - B)$$
$$7A = 56 \qquad\qquad\quad 2B = 60 - 3B$$
$$A = 8 \qquad\qquad\qquad 5B = 60$$
$$B = 12$$

### D. You Must Start Somewhere!

**Answer:** There are many solutions:
2 kg at 5 cm, 5 kg at 30 cm; 3 kg at 80 cm, 4 kg at 75 cm;
2 kg at 10 cm, 5 kg at 30 cm; 4 kg at 70 cm, 3 kg at 100 cm

**Solution:**

You can use the guess-and-test strategy to find possible solutions. To check the first one, use the formula

$$M_2 d_2 + M_1 d_1 = M_3 d_3 + M_4 d_4:$$
$$2 \cdot 45 + 5 \cdot 20 = 3 \cdot 30 + 4 \cdot 25$$
$$90 + 100 = 90 + 100$$
$$190 = 190$$

### Problem Set 7
### DISTANCE EQUALS RATE TIMES TIME

#### A. Burning the Midnight Oil

An overzealous student burns the candle at both ends. One night he lights the top and the bottom of a 10-in. candle at the same time. If the top flame burns at a speed of 1.4 in./h and the bottom flame burns at a rate of 2.1 in./h, how far from the top do the flames meet?

#### B. I Knew It Was Too Hard!

On an algebra test 39 more pupils passed than failed. On a new test, 7 who had passed the first test failed, and one third of those who failed on the first test passed the second test. As a result, 31 more passed the second test than failed it. What was the record of passing and failing on the first test?

#### C. To the Victor Goes . . .

In a Grand Prix automobile race, Rapid Robert averaged 90 mph for the first half of the course and 110 mph for the second half of the course. Steady Eddy maintained a constant speed of 100 mph throughout the race. Who won the race?

## 7-A BURNING THE MIDNIGHT OIL

An overzealous student burns the candle at both ends. One night he lights the top and the bottom of a 10-in. candle at the same time. If the top flame burns at a speed of 1.4 in./h and the bottom flame burns at a rate of 2.1 in./h, how far from the top do the flames meet?

### 7-B I KNEW IT WAS TOO HARD!

On an algebra test 39 more pupils passed than failed. On a new test, 7 who had passed the first test failed, and one third of those who failed on the first test passed the second test. As a result, 31 more passed the second test than failed it. What was the record of passing and failing on the first test?

### 7-C  TO THE VICTOR GOES . . .

In a Grand Prix automobile race, Rapid Robert averaged 90 mph for the first half of the course and 110 mph for the second half of the course. Steady Eddy maintained a constant speed of 100 mph throughout the race. Who won the race?

### 7-D MAKE UP YOUR MIND

An object moved in one direction for
8 seconds at a constant speed. It reversed
direction for 3 seconds with its rate doubled
and then reversed direction again for
1 second at 40% of its initial speed. Find the
three speeds if the object was 9.6 m from its
start at the end of 12 seconds.

## Problem Set 7
## ANSWERS AND SOLUTIONS

### A. Burning the Midnight Oil

**Answer:** 4 in.

**Solution:**

Let $x$ = distance from the top. Then $10 - x$ = distance from the bottom.

$$x = 1.4t \qquad\qquad 10 - x = 2.1t$$

$$\frac{x}{1.4} = \qquad\qquad \frac{10 - x}{2.1} = t$$

$$\frac{x}{1.4} = \frac{10 - x}{2.1}$$

$$2.1x = 14 - 1.4x$$

$$3.5x = 14$$

$$x = 4$$

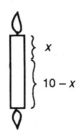

### B. I Knew It Was Too Hard!

**Answer:** 48 passed, 9 failed

**Solution:**

Let $x$ = number that failed the first test; then $x + 39$ = number that passed the first test; $x - \frac{1}{3}x + 7$ = number that failed the new test; and $x + \frac{1}{3}x + 32$ = number that passed the new test.

number passing new test = number failing new test plus 31

$$x + \frac{1}{3}x + 32 = x - \frac{1}{3}x + 7 + 31$$

$$\frac{2}{3}x = 6$$

$$x = 9$$

### C. To the Victor Goes . . .

**Answer:** Steady Eddy

**Solution:**

Let $d$ = total distance for the race, $t_R$ = time for Rapid Robert, and $t_E$ = time for Steady Eddy.

$$t_E = \frac{d}{100}$$

$$t_R \text{ for first half of race} = \frac{d/2}{90} = \frac{d}{180}$$

$$t_R \text{ for second half of race} = \frac{d/2}{110} = \frac{d}{220}$$

$$t_R = \frac{d}{180} + \frac{d}{220} = \frac{d}{20}\left(\frac{1}{9} + \frac{1}{11}\right) = \frac{d}{20} \cdot \frac{20}{99} = \frac{d}{99}$$

$$\frac{d}{100} < \frac{d}{99}, \text{ so Steady Eddy wins.}$$

### D. Make Up Your Mind

**Answer:** 4 m/s, 8m/s, 1.6 m/s

**Solution:**

Let $x$ = original speed of object in meters per second (m/s); then $2x$ = rate of speed when direction is reversed and $0.4x$ = rate of speed in original direction.

$$8x - 6x + 0.4x = 9.6$$

$$2.4x = 9.6$$

$$x = 4$$

## Problem Set 8
## PROBLEMS INVOLVING FACTORS OF NUMBERS

### A. Good Things Come in Pairs

Find the numbers from the set 1, 2, 3, 4, . . . , 50 that have
**a.** an odd number of factors
**b.** exactly two factors

### B. Back and Forth

The 10-by-10 Go board shown here was left in the math office. The first student placed a white Go tile on each number. The second student changed the white tiles on the even numbers to black. The third changed the tiles (from black to white or white to black) on numbers that are multiples of three. The fourth student changed the tiles (from black to white or white to black) on numbers that are multiples of four, the fifth did the same for tiles on multiples of five, and so on. After 100 students pass the Go board, which numbers will be covered with white tiles?

| 1 | 2 | 3 | 4 | 5 | 6 | 7 | 8 | 9 | 10 |
|----|----|----|----|----|----|----|----|----|-----|
| 11 | 12 | 13 | 14 | 15 | 16 | 17 | 18 | 19 | 20 |
| 21 | 22 | 23 | 24 | 25 | 26 | 27 | 28 | 29 | 30 |
| 31 | 32 | 33 | 34 | 35 | 36 | 37 | 38 | 39 | 40 |
| 41 | 42 | 43 | 44 | 45 | 46 | 47 | 48 | 49 | 50 |
| 51 | 52 | 53 | 54 | 55 | 56 | 57 | 58 | 59 | 60 |
| 61 | 62 | 63 | 64 | 65 | 66 | 67 | 68 | 69 | 70 |
| 71 | 72 | 73 | 74 | 75 | 76 | 77 | 78 | 79 | 80 |
| 81 | 82 | 83 | 84 | 85 | 86 | 87 | 88 | 89 | 90 |
| 91 | 92 | 93 | 94 | 95 | 96 | 97 | 98 | 99 | 100 |

### C. Good Things Come in Little Packages

Find the smallest whole number that has exactly 12 factors.

### 8-A  GOOD THINGS COME IN PAIRS

Find the numbers from the set 1, 2, 3, 4, . . . ,
50 that have
**a.** an odd number of factors
**b.** exactly two factors

## 8-B  BACK AND FORTH

The 10-by-10 Go board shown here was left in the math office. The first student placed a white Go tile on each number. The second student changed the white tiles on the even numbers to black. The third changed the tiles (from black to white or white to black) on numbers that are multiples of three. The fourth student changed the tiles (from black to white or white to black) on numbers that are multiples of four, the fifth did the same for tiles on multiples of five, and so on. After 100 students pass the Go board, which numbers will be covered with white tiles?

| 1 | 2 | 3 | 4 | 5 | 6 | 7 | 8 | 9 | 10 |
|----|----|----|----|----|----|----|----|----|-----|
| 11 | 12 | 13 | 14 | 15 | 16 | 17 | 18 | 19 | 20 |
| 21 | 22 | 23 | 24 | 25 | 26 | 27 | 28 | 29 | 30 |
| 31 | 32 | 33 | 34 | 35 | 36 | 37 | 38 | 39 | 40 |
| 41 | 42 | 43 | 44 | 45 | 46 | 47 | 48 | 49 | 50 |
| 51 | 52 | 53 | 54 | 55 | 56 | 57 | 58 | 59 | 60 |
| 61 | 62 | 63 | 64 | 65 | 66 | 67 | 68 | 69 | 70 |
| 71 | 72 | 73 | 74 | 75 | 76 | 77 | 78 | 79 | 80 |
| 81 | 82 | 83 | 84 | 85 | 86 | 87 | 88 | 89 | 90 |
| 91 | 92 | 93 | 94 | 95 | 96 | 97 | 98 | 99 | 100 |

### 8-C  GOOD THINGS COME IN LITTLE PACKAGES

Find the smallest whole number that has
exactly 12 factors.

### 8-D ORDER FROM CHAOS

Find the five different numbers *a*, *b*, *c*, *d*, and *e* that will make all the following conditions true:

$a(b + c + d + e) = 128$

$b(a + c + d + e) = 155$

$c(a + b + d + e) = 203$

$d(a + b + c + e) = 243$

$e(a + b + c + d) = 275$

## Problem Set 8
## ANSWERS AND SOLUTIONS

### A. Good Things Come in Pairs

**Answer:** **a.** 1, 4, 9, 16, 25, 36, 49; **b.** 2, 3, 5, 7, 11, 13, 17, 19, 23, 29, 31, 37, 41, 43, 47

**Solution:**

**a.** Only numbers that are perfect squares have an odd number of factors.

**b.** A prime number has exactly two factors, 1 and the number itself.

### B. Back and Forth

**Answer:** 1, 4, 9, 16, 25, 36, 49, 64, 81, 100

**Solution:**

In solving this problem, the key is to realize that, including the person who placed the tile, each tile that was touched an even number of times would be left with the black side of the tile up. Those touched an odd number of times would have the white side up. Since all perfect squares have an odd number of factors, the tiles on those squares are the ones with the white side up.

### C. Good Things Come in Little Packages

**Answer:** 60

**Solution:**

To find quickly how many factors a number has, you need to look at that number in its prime factored form. Look at the exponents and apply the general multiplication property of counting. For example, the number $2^3 \cdot 3^2$ will have 12 factors, since it has 4 factors involving 2 ($2^3$, $2^2$, $2^1$, $2^0$) and 3 factors involving 3 ($3^2$, $3^1$, $3^0$). Listing all pairs will give the 12 factors of $2^3 \cdot 3^2$. The numbers to consider are ones such that the product of each exponent + 1 gives 12. $x^{11}$, $x^3 \cdot y^2$, $x^5 \cdot y$, and $x^2 \cdot y \cdot z$ are all possible choices. Using the smallest primes gives choices of $2^{11}$, $2^3 \cdot 3^2$, $2^5 \cdot 3$, and $2^2 \cdot 3 \cdot 5$. The smallest possible number is $2^2 \cdot 3 \cdot 5$, or 60.

### D. Order from Chaos

**Answer:** 4, 5, 7, 9, 11

**Solution:**

Factoring each product yields

$$a(b + c + d + e) = 2 \cdot 64 \text{ or } 4 \cdot 32 \text{ or } 8 \cdot 16 = 128$$
$$b(a + c + d + e) = 5 \cdot 31 = 155$$
$$c(a + b + d + e) = 7 \cdot 29 = 203$$
$$d(a + b + c + e) = 3 \cdot 81 \text{ or } 9 \cdot 27 = 243$$
$$e(a + b + c + d) = 5 \cdot 55 \text{ or } 11 \cdot 25 = 275$$

The products $5 \cdot 31$ and $7 \cdot 29$ lead not only to $b = 5$ and $c = 7$ but also to the fact that the sum of the five numbers is 36. Looking for factor pairs whose sum is 36 yields the other three solutions.

## Problem Set 9
## EXAMINING PATTERNS

### A. Déjà Vu

In 1980 I began collecting calendars and I have done so every year since. I will cease collecting when every subsequent year can be served by at least one of the calendars I have already collected. What is the last year in which I must collect a calendar?

### B. It's About Time

One electronic device makes a "bip" each 60 seconds. Another electronic device makes a "bip" each 62 seconds. They both "bip" at 10:00 AM. What time will it be when they will next make a "bip" together?

### C. One Way Is as Good as Another

Six problems (numbered 1 to 6) are set for a mathematics test. A student can score 0, 1, 2, or 3 points for each problem. Find the number of ways to score a total of 15 points for the six problems.

### 9-A DÉJÀ VU

In 1980 I began collecting calendars and I have done so every year since. I will cease collecting when every subsequent year can be served by at least one of the calendars I have already collected. What is the last year in which I must collect a calendar?

## 9-B  IT'S ABOUT TIME

One electronic device makes a "bip" each 60 seconds. Another electronic device makes a "bip" each 62 seconds. They both "bip" at 10:00 AM. What time will it be when they will next make a "bip" together?

### 9-C ONE WAY IS AS GOOD AS ANOTHER

Six problems (numbered 1 to 6) are set for a mathematics test. A student can score 0, 1, 2, or 3 points for each problem. Find the number of ways to score a total of 15 points for the six problems.

### 9-D  BUT I WAS TRYING TO BE FAIR

At a party, Kyra placed 8 saucers around a rectangular table, as shown in the diagram. She placed 32 mints in the 8 saucers so that there was a total of 12 mints along each side of the table. Scott, her brother, said, "I can pick up the 32 mints, add 12 more, and place the 44 mints in the eight saucers so that there will still be 12 mints along each side of the table." Show how he can do this.

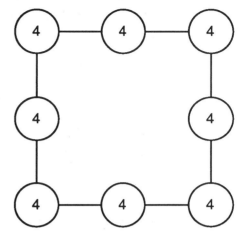

# Problem Set 9
# ANSWERS AND SOLUTIONS

## A. Déjà Vu

**Answer:** 2004

**Solution:**

A nonleap year of 365 days that begins on Monday ends on Tuesday; the second year begins on Tuesday and ends on Wednesday; and so on. A leap year that starts on Monday ends on Wednesday; the next leap year starts on Tuesday and ends on Thursday; and so on. 1980 was a leap year that started on Saturday and ended on Monday. A list of the years follows:

| | | | | |
|---|---|---|---|---|
| **1980** | S$_{Sa}$ E$_M$ | 1993 | S$_M$ E$_{Tu}$ | S=starts |
| 1981 | S$_{Tu}$ E$_W$ | 1994 | S$_W$ E$_{Th}$ | E=ends |
| 1982 | S$_{Th}$ E$_F$ | 1995 | S$_F$ E$_{Sa}$ | |
| 1983 | S$_{Sa}$ E$_{Su}$ | **1996** | S$_{Su}$ E$_{Tu}$ | |
| **1984** | S$_M$ E$_W$ | 1997 | S$_W$ E$_{Th}$ | |
| 1985 | S$_{Th}$ E$_F$ | 1998 | S$_F$ E$_{Sa}$ | |
| 1986 | S$_{Sa}$ E$_{Su}$ | 1999 | S$_{Su}$ E$_M$ | |
| 1987 | S$_M$ E$_{Tu}$ | **2000** | S$_{Tu}$ E$_{Th}$ | |
| **1988** | S$_W$ E$_F$ | 2001 | S$_F$ E$_{Sa}$ | |
| 1989 | S$_{Sa}$ E$_{Su}$ | 2002 | S$_{Su}$ E$_M$ | |
| 1990 | S$_M$ E$_{Tu}$ | 2003 | S$_{Tu}$ E$_W$ | |
| 1991 | S$_W$ E$_{Th}$ | **2004** | S$_{Th}$ E$_{Sa}$ | |
| **1992** | S$_F$ E$_{Su}$ | | | |

## B. It's About Time

**Answer:** 10:31 AM

**Solution:**

This problem involves finding the least common multiple of 60 and 62.

$60 = 2^2 \cdot 3 \cdot 5$

$62 = 2 \cdot 31$

$LCM = 2^2 \cdot 3 \cdot 5 \cdot 31 = 1860$

They will next "bip" together after 1860 seconds, or 31 minutes.

## C. One Way Is as Good as Another

**Answer:** 56 ways

**Solution:**

There are three methods of earning a total of 15 points: 3 points on three questions and 2 points on the other three questions (Case 1); 3 points on four questions, 1 point on one, and 2 points on the other one (Case 2); or 3 points on five questions and 0 on the sixth (Case 3).

Case 1: If the questions are numbered 1–6, we need to list only those questions worth 3 points. They are

| | | | | | | | | | |
|---|---|---|---|---|---|---|---|---|---|
| 123 | 134 | 145 | 156 | 234 | 245 | 256 | 345 | 356 | 456 |
| 124 | 135 | 146 | | 235 | 246 | | 346 | | |
| 125 | 136 | | | 236 | | | | | |
| 126 | | | | | | | | | |

Thus, there are 20 ways.

Case 2: Any of the 6 problems could have earned 1 point, with one of the other five earning 2 points, so there are 6 · 5, or 30 ways.

Case 3: Any of the 6 problems could have earned 0 points; the remaining 5 problems would earn 3 points. Thus, there are 6 ways.

The total is 20 + 30 + 6, or 56 ways.

## D. But I Was Trying to Be Fair

**Answer:** See Solution.

**Solution:**

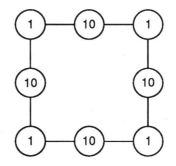

## Problem Set 10
## FACTORS AND EXPONENTS

### A. It Takes Two to Tango

In how many zeros does 150! end?
(! means factorial: $5! = 5 \cdot 4 \cdot 3 \cdot 2 \cdot 1$)

### B. The More the Merrier

What is the largest number that can be obtained as the product of positive integers whose sum is 100?

Examples:

$50 + 50 = 100$, $50^2 = 2500$

$25 + 25 + 25 + 25 = 100$, $25^4 = 390{,}625$

$50 + 10 + 10 + 10 + 10 + 10 = 100$,
$50(10^5) = 5{,}000{,}000$

$\underbrace{5 + 5 + \cdots + 5}_{20} = 100$, $5^{20} \approx 9.54(10^{13})$

$\underbrace{5 + 5 + \cdots + 5}_{10} + \underbrace{2 + 2 + \cdots + 2}_{25} = 100$,

$(5^{10})(2^{25}) \approx 3.28(10^{14})$

### C. It's About Sharing

How many factors does $a^2 b^3 c^4$ have? (a, b, and c represent different prime numbers.)

### 10-A  IT TAKES TWO TO TANGO

In how many zeros does 150! end?
(! means factorial: $5! = 5 \cdot 4 \cdot 3 \cdot 2 \cdot 1$)

© Dale Seymour Publications

## 10-B  THE MORE THE MERRIER

What is the largest number that can be obtained as the product of positive integers whose sum is 100?

Examples:

$50 + 50 = 100$, $50^2 = 2500$

$25 + 25 + 25 + 25 = 100$, $25^4 = 390,625$

$50 + 10 + 10 + 10 + 10 + 10 = 100$,
$50(10^5) = 5,000,000$

$\underbrace{5 + 5 + \cdots + 5}_{20} = 100$, $5^{20} \approx 9.54(10^{13})$

$\underbrace{5 + 5 + \cdots + 5}_{10} + \underbrace{2 + 2 + \cdots + 2}_{25} = 100$,

$(5^{10})(2^{25}) \approx 3.28(10^{14})$

### 10-C IT'S ABOUT SHARING

How many factors does $a^2b^3c^4$ have? ($a$, $b$, and $c$ represent different prime numbers.)

### 10-D. JACK AND THE FLOWER STALK

A sunflower plant was purchased with the following growth guarantee. After being planted, on the first day it would grow 100 mm. On the second day its height would increase by one half (50%), on the third day by one third, on the fourth day by one fourth, and so on. Assuming that the plant actually grows according to the guarantee, how many days would it take for it to reach its maximum height of 5000 mm?

# Problems Set 10
# ANSWERS AND SOLUTIONS

## A. It Takes Two to Tango

**Answer:** 37

**Solution:**

The number of zeros at the end of a product is determined by factors of 2 and 5. Since there are fewer factors of 5 than factors of 2 in 150, determining the number of factors of 5 determines the answer. In 150!, there are 30 multiples of 5 for 30 5s, 6 multiples of $5^2$ for 6 more 5s, and 1 multiple of $5^3$ for an additional 5, making a total of 37.

## B. The More the Merrier

**Answer:** $3^{32} \cdot 2^2$

**Solution:**

It appears that the more numbers you can multiply together the better. $2^{50} = 1.13 \times 10^{15}$. Since $3^2 > 2^3$, it is easy to show $3^{33} \cdot 1 > 2^{50}$. So, $3^{33} \cdot 1 = 5.56 \times 10^{15}$. The final answer of $3^{32} \cdot 2^2$ is found because $2^2 > 3^1 \cdot 1$.

## C. It's About Sharing

**Answer:** 60

**Solution:**

This problem is related to the general multiplication principle because $a^2$ has 3 factors: $a^2$, $a$, and 1; $b^3$ has 4 factors: $b^3$, $b^2$, $b$, and 1; $c^4$ has 5 factors: $c^4$, $c^3$, $c^2$, $c$, and 1. $(a^2 + a + 1)(b^3 + b^2 + b + 1)(c^4 + c^3 + c^2 + c + 1)$ will give all the possible factors.

## D. Jack and the Flower Stalk

**Answer:** 99 days

**Solution:**

The table reveals that after the first day the plant grows at a rate of 50 mm per day. Solving the equation $50d = 4900$ leads to $d = 98$. It would take the plant 99 days to grow to its maximum height of 5000 mm.

| Days | Height |
|------|--------|
| 1 | 100 |
| 2 | $100 + \frac{1}{2}(100) = 150$ |
| 3 | $150 + \frac{1}{3}(150) = 200$ |
| 4 | $200 + \frac{1}{4}(200) = 250$ |

## Problem Set 11
## PASCAL'S TRIANGLE

### A. Patterns Galore

The array shows the first four rows of
the triangle attributed to the French
mathematician Blaise Pascal. Study the
triangle and determine the entries in the
tenth row.

### B. Expansion Sale

Without multiplying out $(x + y)^{10}$ the long way,
see if you can write out the product. (*Hint:* The
solution to Problem 10-A can really help.)

### C. Nothing Ventured, Nothing Gained

Find the sum of the numerical coefficients
of $(x - y)^{10}$.

### 11-A  PATTERNS GALORE

The array shows the first four rows of the triangle attributed to the French mathematician Blaise Pascal. Study the triangle and determine the entries in the tenth row.

```
            1
          1   1
        1   2   1
      1   3   3   1
    1   4   6   4   1
```

## 11-B EXPANSION SALE

Without multiplying out $(x + y)^{10}$ the long way, see if you can write out the product. (*Hint:* The solution to Problem 10-A can really help.)

### 11-C  NOTHING VENTURED, NOTHING GAINED

Find the sum of the numerical coefficients
of $(x - y)^{10}$.

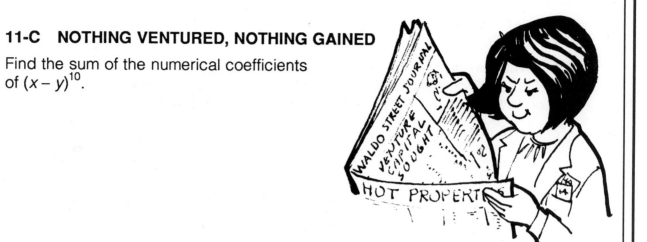

### 11-D MORE POWER TO YOU

Find the sum of the numerical coefficients of $(x + y)^n$. (*Hint:* Find the sum of the coefficients of $(x + y)^1$, $(x + y)^2$, and so on.)

# Problem Set 11
## ANSWERS AND SOLUTIONS

### A. Patterns Galore

**Answer:** 1, 10, 45, 120, 210, 252, 120, 45, 10, 1
**Solution:**

```
            1    5   10   10    5    1
         1    6   15   20   15    6    1
      1    7   21   35   35   21    7    1
   1    8   28   56   70   56   28    8    1
1    9   36   84  126  126   84   36    9    1
1   10   45  120  210  252  210  120   45   10    1
```

### B. Expansion Sale

**Answer:** $x^{10} + 10x^9y + 45x^8y^2 + 120x^7y^3 + 210x^6y^4 + 252x^5y^5 + 210x^4y^6 + 120x^3y^7 + 45x^2y^8 + 10xy^9 + y^{10}$

**Solution:**

By expanding $(x + y)^1$, $(x + y)^2$, $(x + y)^3$, and so on, it becomes apparent that the coefficients in each expression are listed in the appropriate row in Pascal's triangle. The pattern of exponents is also easy to see, since the degree of each term is the same as the power.

### C. Nothing Ventured, Nothing Gained

**Answer:** 0
**Solution:**
Expanding $(x + y)^{10}$ and $(x - y)^{10}$ gives the same numbers, but the signs of the terms alternate between + and –. To find the sum of the coefficients of $(x - y)^{10}$, the sum of $1 - 10 + 45 - 120 + 210 - 252 + 210 - 120 + 45 - 10 + 1$ must be found.

### D. More Power to You

**Answer:** $2^n$
**Solution:**
Examining the first few rows of Pascal's triangle is enough to prove this answer.

$(x + y)^1 = 1x + 1y$  Sum of coeff. $= 2 = 2^1$
$(x + y)^2 = 1x^2 + 2xy + 1y^2$  Sum of coeff. $= 4 = 2^2$
$(x + y)^3 = 1x^3 + 3x^2y + 3xy^2 + 1y^3$  Sum of coeff. $= 8 = 2^3$

```
        1    1
      1    2    1
    1    3    3    1
  1    4    6    4    1
           .
           .
           .
```

### Problem Set 12
### FACTORIZATION

#### A. Calculating Combinations

Write the prime factorization of 22,438,769.

#### B. Let's Make It a Threesome

Find three positive integers whose sum is 30 and whose product is 840.

#### C. Leftovers Again!

What is the remainder when $3^{777777}$ is divided by 7?

### 12-A CALCULATING COMBINATIONS

Write the prime factorization of 22,438,769.

### 12-B  LET'S MAKE IT A THREESOME

Find three positive integers whose sum is 30 and whose product is 840.

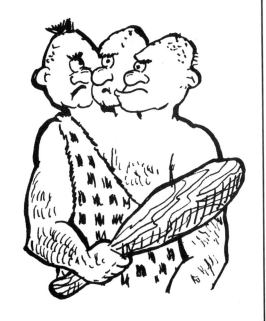

### 12-C LEFTOVERS AGAIN!

What is the remainder when $3^{777777}$ is divided by 7?

### 12-D  THOSE WERE THE DAYS

Three ex-teenagers find that the product of
their ages is 26,390. Find the sum of their
ages.

## Problem Set 12
## ANSWERS AND SOLUTIONS

### A. Calculating Combinations

**Answer:** $53 \times 67 \times 71 \times 89$

**Solution:**

This problem is a good exercise on the calculator. A table of primes is very useful.

### B. Let's Make It a Threesome

**Answer:** 6, 10, 14

**Solution:**

Factoring 840 into primes gives $2 \cdot 2 \cdot 2 \cdot 3 \cdot 5 \cdot 7$. Choosing pairs of factors by trial and error leads to the solution.

### C. Leftovers Again!

**Answer:** 6

**Solution:**

Making a table of powers of 3s and then dividing by 7 to find the remainder presents a repeating pattern. Once the pattern is established, the problem becomes one of seeing how 777,777 fits in the pattern.

$$3^0 = 1 \div 7 = 0 \cdot 7 + 1$$
$$3^1 = 3 \div 7 = 0 \cdot 7 + 3$$
$$3^2 = 9 \div 7 = 1 \cdot 7 + 2$$
$$3^3 = 27 \div 7 = 3 \cdot 7 + 6$$
$$3^4 = 81 \div 7 = 11 \cdot 7 + 4$$
$$3^5 = 243 \div 7 = 34 \cdot 7 + 5$$
$$3^6 = 729 \div 7 = 104 \cdot 7 + 1$$
$$3^7 = 2187 \div 7 = 312 \cdot 7 + 3$$
$$3^8 = 6561 \div 7 = 937 \cdot 7 + 2$$

It appears that 3 raised to a multiple of 6 results in a remainder of 1. Dividing 777,777 by 6 leaves a remainder of 3, meaning $3^{777777} = 3^{(129629)6} \cdot 3^3$. Since $3^3$ leaves a remainder of 6, so will $3^{777777}$.

### D. Those Were the Days

**Answer:** $26 + 29 + 35 = 90$

**Solution:**

Factoring 26,390 as a product of primes gives $2 \cdot 5 \cdot 7 \cdot 13 \cdot 29$. Since each person is an ex-teenager, we are looking for 3 factors, all greater than 19, that give 26,390 as a product. The ages must be 26 ($2 \cdot 13$), 29, and 35 ($5 \cdot 7$), as any other combination leaves one factor less than 20.

## Problem Set 13
## POWERS OF NUMBERS

### A. Different Strokes for Different Folks

Find the difference between the smallest perfect square larger than one million and the largest perfect square smaller than one million. (A perfect square has a square root that is an integer.)

### B. We Want to Be Different

Find all pairs of positive integers $x$ and $y$ so that $x^2 - y^2 = 48$.

### C. Tower of Power

Joe Lucky recently won the California lottery. The amount of money that he won just happens to be the smallest number of cents (other than 1¢) that is a perfect square, a perfect cube, and a perfect fifth power. How much money did he actually win?

## 13-A DIFFERENT STROKES FOR DIFFERENT FOLKS

Find the difference between the smallest perfect square larger than one million and the largest perfect square smaller than one million. (A perfect square has a square root that is an integer.)

### 13-B  WE WANT TO BE DIFFERENT

Find all pairs of positive integers $x$ and $y$ so that $x^2 - y^2 = 48$.

## 13-C  TOWER OF POWER

Joe Lucky recently won the California lottery. The amount of money that he won just happens to be the smallest number of cents (other than 1¢) that is a perfect square, a perfect cube, and a perfect fifth power. How much money did he actually win?

## 13-D  3-D GLASSES HELP!

The figure gives a geometric representation that shows why $(x + y)^2 = x^2 + 2xy + y^2$. Draw a geometric figure to show that $(x + y)^3 = x^3 + 3x^2y + 3xy^2 + y^3$.

|  | $x$ | $y$ |
|---|---|---|
| $x$ | $x^2$ | $xy$ |
| $y$ | $xy$ | $y^2$ |

# Problem Set 13
## ANSWERS AND SOLUTIONS

### A. Different Strokes for Different Folks

**Answer:** 4000

**Solution:**

Although this problem can be solved by using a table of perfect squares or a computer, a better algebraic solution results from the fact that $1,000,000 = 1000^2$. The smallest perfect square larger than 1,000,000 is $1001^2$, whereas the largest perfect square smaller than 1,000,000 is $999^2$. $1001^2 - 999^2$ gives the proper solution. Factoring $1001^2 - 999^2$ gives

$(1001 + 999)(1001 - 999) = 2000 \cdot 2 = 4000$

### B. We Want to Be Different

**Answer:** (7, 1), (8, 4), (13, 11)

**Solution:**

The solution (7, 1) can be found easily, since 48 is 1 less than the perfect square 49. The others can be found by using a factoring technique based on the difference of two squares.

$m^2 - n^2 = (m + n)(m - n) \qquad m + n > m - n$

$$
\begin{aligned}
(m + n)(m - n) &= 48 \cdot 1 \\
&= 24 \cdot 2 \\
&= 16 \cdot 3 \\
&= 12 \cdot 4 \\
&= 8 \cdot 6
\end{aligned}
$$

Using each of the factorizations of 48 leads to five systems of equations that can be solved easily:

| $m + n = 48$ | $m + n = 24$ | $m + n = 16$ | $m + n = 12$ | $m + n = 8$ |
|---|---|---|---|---|
| $m - n = 1$ | $m - n = 2$ | $m - n = 3$ | $m - n = 4$ | $m - n = 6$ |
| $2m = 49$ | $2m = 26$ | $2m = 19$ | $2m = 16$ | $2m = 14$ |
| $m = \dfrac{49}{2}$ | $m = 13$ | $m = \dfrac{19}{2}$ | $m = 8$ | $m = 7$ |
| not an integer | $n = 11$ | not an integer | $n = 4$ | $n = 1$ |

### C. Tower of Power

**Answer:** \$10,737,418.24

**Solution:**

Since the smallest number is needed, powers of 2 are desired; $2^2$ is the smallest square, $2^3$ is the smallest cube, and $2^5$ is the smallest perfect fifth.

$2^2, 2^4, 2^6, 2^8, 2^{10}, \ldots$ are all perfect squares
$2^3, 2^6, 2^9, 2^{12}, \ldots$ are all perfect cubes
$2^5, 2^{10}, 2^{15}, 2^{20}, \ldots$ are all perfect fifths

The desired result is the smallest number in each of the three sets. That number is $((2^2)^3)^5$, or $2^{30}$.

### D. 3-D Glasses Help!

**Answer:** See Solution.

**Solution:**

The $x^3$ and $y^3$ pieces are shown as bold lines in the figure.

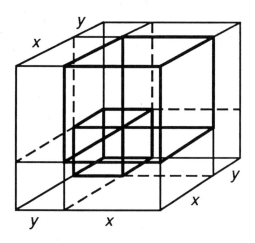

## Problem Set 14
## NUMBER THEORY

### A. Cast Out Imposters

**1.** If an integer is a perfect square, determine which of the digits 0–9 cannot be in the units place.

**2.** Repeat Part 1 if the integer is a perfect cube.

**3.** Repeat Part 1 if the integer is a perfect fourth.

### B. Sum Fun

**1.** List all the two-digit numbers that are divisible by the product of their digits.

**2.** List all the two-digit numbers that are divisible by the sum of their digits.

### C. Odd Man Out

An integer is said to be even if 2 is a factor of the number and odd otherwise. If *ABCD* is the base *b* representation of a number *n*, under what circumstances is *n* odd if

**a.** $b = 10$

**b.** $b = 2$

**c.** $b = 3$

**d.** $b = 5$

### 14-A  CAST OUT IMPOSTERS

1. If an integer is a perfect square, determine which of the digits 0–9 cannot be in the units place.
2. Repeat Part 1 if the integer is a perfect cube.
3. Repeat Part 1 if the integer is a perfect fourth.

### 14-B  SUM FUN

1. List all the two-digit numbers that are divisible by the product of their digits.
2. List all the two-digit numbers that are divisible by the sum of their digits.

### 14-C  ODD MAN OUT

An integer is said to be even if 2 is a factor of the number and odd otherwise. If *ABCD* is the base *b* representation of a number *n* , under what circumstances is *n* odd if

**a.** $b = 10$
**b.** $b = 2$
**c.** $b = 3$
**d.** $b = 5$

### 14-D  ODDS AND EVENS

Consider the sequence defined by
$$S(n) = 1 - 2 + 3 - 4 + 5 - 6 + \cdots + (-1)^{n-1}n$$

$S(1) = 1$
$S(2) = 1 - 2 = -1$
$S(3) = 1 - 2 + 3 = 2$
$S(4) = 1 - 2 + 3 - 4 = -2$

.
.
.

$S(10) = 1 - 2 + 3 + \cdots + 9 - 10 = -5$
Find $S(30) + S(40) + S(75)$.

# Problem Set 14
## ANSWERS AND SOLUTIONS

### A. Cast Out Imposters

**Answer:** **1.** 2, 3, 7, 8

**2.** Any of 0–9 may be in the units spot

**3.** 2, 3, 7, 8

**Solution:**

For each of these parts, consider the numbers 1–10, and square, cube, and raise each to the fourth.

| | | |
|---|---|---|
| $1^2 = 1$ | $1^3 = 1$ | Since fourth powers are |
| $2^2 = 4$ | $2^3 = 8$ | squares, the same |
| $3^2 = 9$ | $3^3 = 27$ | digits will appear as |
| $4^2 = 16$ | $4^3 = 64$ | for squares. |
| $5^2 = 25$ | $5^3 = 125$ | |
| $6^2 = 36$ | $6^3 = 216$ | |
| $7^2 = 49$ | $7^3 = 343$ | |
| $8^2 = 64$ | $8^3 = 512$ | |
| $9^2 = 81$ | $9^3 = 729$ | |
| $10^2 = 100$ | $10^3 = 1000$ | |
| From the digits 0–9, 2, 3, 7, and 8 are missing. | All digits from 0–9 are possible. | |

### B. Sum Fun

**Answer:** **1.** 11, 12, 15, 24, 36

**2.** 10, 12, 18, 20, 21, 24, 27, 30, 36, 40, 42, 45, 48, 50, 63, 70, 72, 80, 81, 84, 90

**Solution:**

For both questions the best way to find a solution is to list the numbers from 10–99 and systematically check each number.

### C. Odd Man Out

**Answer:** **a.** The number is odd if the units digit is 1, 3, 5, 7, or 9.

**b.** In base 2, a number is odd if the units digit is 1.

**c.** In base 3, a number is odd if the sum of the digits is an odd number in base 10.

**d.** In base 5, a number is odd if the sum of the digits is an odd number in base 10.

**Solution:**

In general, if the base is even, a number is odd if the units digit is an odd number in base 10. If the base is odd, then a number is odd if the sum of the digits is an odd number in base 10.

### D. Odds and Evens

**Answer:** 3

**Solution:**

Examining patterns leads to the following generalizations:

If $n$ is even, $S(n) = -\dfrac{n}{2}$.

If $n$ is odd, $S(n) = \dfrac{n+1}{2}$.

Using this generalization,

$S(30) = -\dfrac{30}{2} = -15$

$S(40) = -\dfrac{40}{2} = -20$

$S(75) = \dfrac{75 + 1}{2} = 38$

$S(30) + S(40) + S(75) = -15 + (-20) + 38 = 3$

### Problem Set 15
### NUMBER THEORY

#### A. 3, 6, 9, 12, Solve It Yourself

The difference between the squares of two consecutive multiples of three is 1989. Show how you found the solution.

#### B. Organized Mayhem

Find three ways to express 1989 as the sum of the squares of three positive integers. Show why each of your solutions works.

#### C. Calculator Not Needed

If $A = (1 - 9 + 8 + 9)^{1989}$ and $C = (1 - 9 + 8 - 9)^{1989}$, find the value of $(1 + 9 + 8 + 9)^{A+C}$.

### 15-A   3, 6, 9, 12, SOLVE IT YOURSELF

The difference between the squares of two consecutive multiples of three is 1989. Show how you found the solution.

## 15-B  ORGANIZED MAYHEM

Find three ways to express 1989 as the sum of the squares of three positive integers. Show why each of your solutions works.

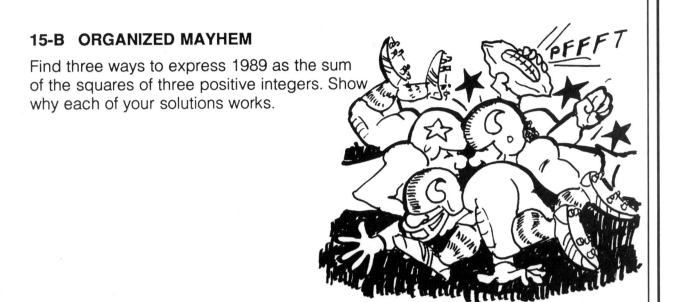

## 15-C  CALCULATOR NOT NEEDED

If $A = (1 - 9 + 8 + 9)^{1989}$ and
$C = (1 - 9 + 8 - 9)^{1989}$, find the
value of $(1 + 9 + 8 + 9)^{A+C}$.

## 15-D  FOILED AGAIN

Find the value of $x$ for which $(1989 - x)^2 = x^2$.

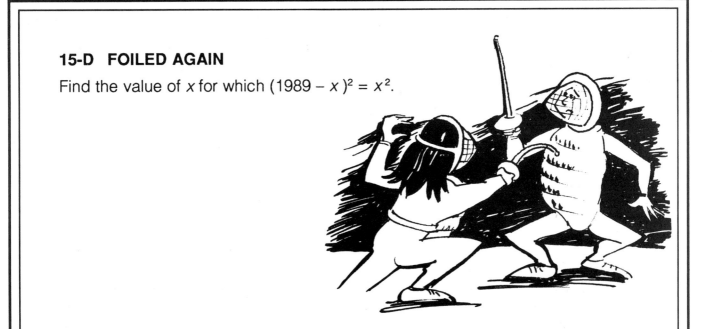

# Problem Set 15
## ANSWERS AND SOLUTIONS

### A. 3, 6, 9, 12, Solve It Yourself

**Answer:** 330 and 333

**Solution:**

Let $n$ = a multiple of 3. Then $n + 3$ = next multiple of three.

$$(n + 3)^2 - n^2 = 1989$$
$$n^2 + 6n + 9 - n^2 = 1989$$
$$6n = 1980$$
$$n = 330$$
$$n + 3 = 333$$

### B. Organized Mayhem

**Answer:** Any three of the following triples are correct:
(2, 7, 44), (9, 12, 42), (10, 17, 40), (12, 18, 39), (4, 23, 38),
(7, 28, 34), (18, 24, 33), (2, 31, 32), (17, 26, 32), (23, 26, 28)

**Solution:**

A table of perfect squares and a calculator with a memory make this problem more manageable. One way to solve is to first subtract the largest perfect square less than 1989 from 1989 and then work with that result to see if there are two perfect squares giving that sum.

$$1989 - 44^2 = 53$$
$$53 = 7^2 + 2^2$$

Therefore, $2^2 + 7^2 + 44^2 = 1989$.

### C. Calculator Not Needed

**Answer:** 1

**Solution:**

$$A = (1 - 9 + 8 + 9)^{1989} = (9)^{1989}$$
$$C = (1 - 9 + 8 - 9)^{1989} = (-9)^{1989}$$
$$A + C = 0$$
$$(1 + 9 + 8 + 9)^0 = 1$$

### D. Foiled Again

**Answer:** 994.5

**Solution 1:**

Expanding $(1989 - x)^2 = x^2$,

$$3,956,121 - 3978x + x^2 = x^2$$
$$3,956,121 = 3978x$$
$$994.5 = x$$

**Solution 2:**

Taking the square root of both sides of $(1989 - x)^2 = x^2$ yields

$$1989 - x = \pm x$$
$$1989 = 2x$$
$$994.5 = x$$

## Problem Set 16
## FACTORING

### A. Groups Are In

Each of the following can be *completely* factored as the product of two or more factors. Show how to factor any two of the following.

$4x^2 - 25y^2 + 4x + 10y$

$x(x + 1)(4x - 5) - 6(x + 1)$

$a^4 - b^4 - 2a^3b + 2ab^3$

$x^3 - x^2 - 9x + 9$

### B. Quadruple Your Pleasure

Around the outside of a rectangular flower bed 4 ft wide and 12 ft long there is a grass border whose width is uniform and whose area is four times the area of the flower bed. Find the width of the border.

### C. Sounds Right to Me

A woman drove her car on a road running due north at a given rate for 6 hours. She continued her trip on an unpaved road due east for 5 hours at a rate 4 mph slower. Had she been able to go to her destination in a straight line from her starting point and at her original rate, she would have taken $7\frac{1}{2}$ hours. Find her rate for the first part of her journey.

### 16-A GROUPS ARE IN

Each of the following can be *completely* factored as the product of two or more factors. Show how to factor any two of the following.

$4x^2 - 25y^2 + 4x + 10y$

$x(x + 1)(4x - 5) - 6(x + 1)$

$a^4 - b^4 - 2a^3b + 2ab^3$

$x^3 - x^2 - 9x + 9$

### 16-B QUADRUPLE YOUR PLEASURE

Around the outside of a rectangular flower bed 4 ft wide and 12 ft long there is a grass border whose width is uniform and whose area is four times the area of the flower bed. Find the width of the border.

## 16-C  SOUNDS RIGHT TO ME

A woman drove her car on a road running due north at a given rate for 6 hours. She continued her trip on an unpaved road due east for 5 hours at a rate 4 mph slower. Had she been able to go to her destination in a straight line from her starting point and at her original rate, she would have taken $7\frac{1}{2}$ hours. Find her rate for the first part of her journey.

### 16-D  ADDING ZERO STILL LEAVES YOU NOTHING

Most first-year algebra teachers stress that you cannot factor the sum of two perfect squares. However, if the circumstances are right, by adding and subtracting the same perfect square, this type of factoring is possible. One of the five choices shown is the correct factorization of $x^2 + 64$. Which one?

**a.** $(x^2 + 8)^2$

**b.** $(x^2 + 8)(x^2 - 8)$

**c.** $(x^2 + 2x + 4)(x^2 - 8x + 16)$

**d.** $(x^2 - 4x + 8)(x^2 + 4x + 8)$

**e.** $(x^2 - 4x + 8)(x^2 - 4x - 8)$

Show, if you can, how to factor $x^4 + 4$.

# Problem Set 16
## ANSWERS AND SOLUTIONS

### A. Groups Are In

**Answer:** $4x^2 - 25y^2 + 4x + 10y = (2x + 5y)(2x - 5y + 2)$;
$a^4 - b^4 - 2a^3b + 2ab^3 = (a - b)^3(a + b)$;
$x(x + 1)(4x - 5) - 6(x + 1) = (x + 1)(x - 2)(4x + 3)$;
$x^3 - x^2 - 9x + 9 = (x - 1)(x + 3)(x - 3)$

**Solution:**
$4x^2 - 25y^2 + 4x + 10y$
$= (2x + 5y)(2x - 5y) + 2(2x + 5y)$
$= (2x + 5y)(2x - 5y + 2)$

$a^4 - b^4 - 2a^3b + 2ab^3$
$= (a^2 - b^2)(a^2 + b^2) - 2ab(a^2 - b^2)$
$= (a^2 - b^2)(a^2 + b^2 - 2ab)$
$= (a + b)(a - b)(a - b)(a - b)$
$= (a - b)^3(a + b)$

$x(x + 1)(4x - 5) - 6(x + 1)$
$= (x + 1)[x(4x - 5) - 6]$
$= (x + 1)(4x^2 - 5x - 6)$
$= (x + 1)(x - 2)(4x + 3)$

$x^3 - x^2 - 9x + 9$
$= x^2(x - 1) - 9(x - 1)$
$= (x - 1)(x^2 - 9)$
$= (x - 1)(x + 3)(x - 3)$

### B. Quadruple Your Pleasure

**Answer:** 4 ft

**Solution:**
Area (combined region) = Area (flower bed) + Area (border)
$(2x + 4)(2x + 12) = 4 \cdot 12 + 4(4 \cdot 12)$
$4(x + 2)(x + 6) = 5(4 \cdot 12)$
$(x + 2)(x + 6) = 60$
$x^2 + 8x + 12 = 60$
$x^2 + 8x - 48 = 0$
$(x + 12)(x - 4) = 0$
$x = 4$

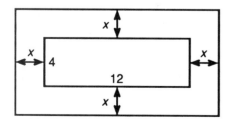

### C. Sounds Right to Me

**Answer:** 40 mph

**Solution:**
Let $x$ = rate going north
$D_{north} = 6x$
$x - 4$ = rate going east
$D_{east} = 5(x - 4)$
$D_{SE} = 7\frac{1}{2}x$

$(6x)^2 + [5(x - 4)]^2 = (7\frac{1}{2}x)^2$
$36x^2 + 25x^2 - 200x + 400 = \dfrac{225}{4}x^2$
$144x^2 + 100x^2 - 800x + 1600 = 225x^2$
$19x^2 - 800x + 1600 = 0$
$(19x - 40)(x - 40) = 0$
$x = 40$ is only reasonable answer

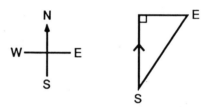

### D. Adding Zero Still Leaves You Nothing

**Answer:** d

**Solution 1:**
By adding and subtracting $16x^2$, $x^4 + 64$ becomes
$x^4 + 16x^2 + 64 - 16x^2$. This polynomial can be factored using the difference of two squares technique.
$x^4 + 16x^2 + 64 - 16x^2 = (x^2 + 8)^2 - (4x)^2$
$= (x^2 + 8 + 4x)(x^2 + 8 - 4x)$
$x^4 + 4 = x^4 + 4x^2 + 4 - 4x^2$
$= (x^2 + 2)^2 - (2x)^2$
$= (x^2 + 2 + 2x)(x^2 + 2 - 2x)$

**Solution 2:**
Students might determine the answer by just multiplying choices.

### Problem Set 17
### FRACTIONS

#### A. Substitutes Are Fair Game

Determine whether the following are equivalent. Explain your answer.

$$\frac{3351^2 - 3347^2}{3350 \cdot 3353 - 3351^2} \quad \text{and} \quad \frac{4351^2 - 4347^2}{4350 \cdot 4353 - 4351^2}$$

#### B. What's Up Comes Down

The sum of two positive numbers equals the sum of the reciprocals of the same two numbers. Find the product of these two numbers.

#### C. How Wise Are You?

If $\dfrac{13x - 6y}{x + 3y} = 3$, find the numerical value of

$\dfrac{x + y}{x - y}$.

## 17-A  SUBSTITUTES ARE FAIR GAME

Determine whether the following are
equivalent. Explain your answer.

$$\frac{3351^2 - 3347^2}{3350 \cdot 3353 - 3351^2} \quad \text{and} \quad \frac{4351^2 - 4347^2}{4350 \cdot 4353 - 4351^2}$$

## 17-B  WHAT'S UP COMES DOWN

The sum of two positive numbers equals the sum of the reciprocals of the same two numbers. Find the product of these two numbers.

### 17-C   HOW WISE ARE YOU?

If $\dfrac{13x - 6y}{x + 3y} = 3$, find the numerical value of

$\dfrac{x + y}{x - y}$.

## 17-D THE PART'S THE THING

Compute each of the following:

**a.** $\left(1 - \dfrac{1}{2^2}\right)$

**b.** $\left(1 - \dfrac{1}{2^2}\right)\left(1 - \dfrac{1}{3^2}\right)$

**c.** $\left(1 - \dfrac{1}{2^2}\right)\left(1 - \dfrac{1}{3^2}\right)\left(1 - \dfrac{1}{4^2}\right)$

**d.** $\left(1 - \dfrac{1}{2^2}\right)\left(1 - \dfrac{1}{3^2}\right)\left(1 - \dfrac{1}{4^2}\right)\left(1 - \dfrac{1}{5^2}\right)$

Without actually computing the result, give a good argument as to what common fraction the following might be.

$$\left(1 - \dfrac{1}{2^2}\right)\left(1 - \dfrac{1}{3^2}\right)\left(1 - \dfrac{1}{4^2}\right)\cdots\left(1 - \dfrac{1}{50^2}\right)$$

## Problem Set 17
## ANSWERS AND SOLUTIONS

### A. Substitutes Are Fair Game

**Answer:** Yes. Both equal 8.

**Solution:**

$$\frac{3351^2 - 3347^2}{3350 \cdot 3353 - 3351^2} \qquad \frac{4351^2 - 4347^2}{4350 \cdot 4353 - 4351^2}$$

Let $x = 3351$:

$$\frac{x^2 - (x-4)^2}{(x-1)(x+2)}$$

Let $x = 4351$:

$$\frac{x^2 - (x-4)^2}{(x-1)(x+2)}$$

$$= \frac{x^2 - x^2 + 8x - 16}{x^2 + x - 2 - x^2}$$

$$= \frac{8(x-2)}{(x-2)}$$

$$= 8$$

### B. What's Up Comes Down

**Answer:** 1

**Solution:**

The sum of the two numbers is $x + y$, whereas the sum of the reciprocals is $\frac{1}{x} + \frac{1}{y} = \frac{x+y}{xy}$. Since the sum of the numbers equals the sum of the reciprocals, $x + y = \frac{x+y}{xy}$. Therefore $xy = \frac{x+y}{x+y}$, or 1.

### C. How Wise Are You?

**Answer:** 5

**Solution:**

$$\frac{13x - 6y}{x + 3y} = 3$$

$$13x - 6y = 3x + 9y$$

$$10x = 15y$$

$$x = \frac{15}{10}y = \frac{3}{2}y$$

$$\frac{x+y}{x-y} = \frac{\frac{3}{2}y + y}{\frac{3}{2}y - y} = \frac{2.5y}{0.5y} = 5$$

### D. The Part's the Thing

**Answer:** a. $\frac{3}{4}$   b. $\frac{2}{3}$   c. $\frac{5}{8}$   d. $\frac{3}{5}$

**Solution:**

This problem can be expressed by this notation:

$$\prod_{i=2}^{n}\left(1 - \frac{1}{i^2}\right) = \left(1 - \frac{1}{2^2}\right)\left(1 - \frac{1}{3^2}\right)\cdots\left(1 - \frac{1}{n^2}\right)$$

The problem explores what happens to the product as the value of $n$ increases. The table shows the solution to a–d.

| $n$ | $\prod_{i=2}^{n}\left(1 - \dfrac{1}{i^2}\right)$ |
|---|---|
| 2 | $\dfrac{3}{4}$ |
| 3 | $\dfrac{3}{4} \cdot \dfrac{8}{9} = \dfrac{2}{3}$ |
| 4 | $\dfrac{2}{3} \cdot \dfrac{15}{16} = \dfrac{5}{8}$ |
| 5 | $\dfrac{5}{8} \cdot \dfrac{24}{25} = \dfrac{3}{5}$ |

Note that if $\dfrac{3}{4}, \dfrac{2}{3}, \dfrac{5}{8}, \dfrac{3}{5} \cdots$ is written as $\dfrac{3}{4}, \dfrac{4}{6}, \dfrac{5}{8}, \dfrac{6}{10} \cdots$, a pattern emerges.

Since $\dfrac{3}{4} = \dfrac{2+1}{2 \cdot 2}, \dfrac{4}{6} = \dfrac{3+1}{2 \cdot 3}$, and $\dfrac{5}{8} = \dfrac{4+1}{2 \cdot 4}$,

then $\dfrac{n+1}{2n}$ describes the product $\displaystyle\prod_{i=2}^{n}\left(1 + \frac{1}{i^2}\right)$ for any $n$.

Thus, $\displaystyle\prod_{i=2}^{\infty}\left(1 - \frac{1}{i^2}\right) = \lim_{n\to\infty} \frac{n+1}{2n} = \frac{1}{2}$.

**Problem Set 18**
**FRACTIONS**

### A. *X* Marks the Spot

Work the following problem without doing a lot of arithmetic.

$$\frac{6831^2 - 6833^2}{(6833)(6832) - (6832)(6837)}$$

### B. The Whole Is Greater Than Its Parts

Unit fractions are fractions that have a numerator of 1 and a denominator of any whole number greater than 1. Can you find five *different* unit fractions whose sum is 1?

$$\frac{1}{a} + \frac{1}{b} + \frac{1}{c} + \frac{1}{d} + \frac{1}{e} = 1, \, a \neq b \neq c \neq d \neq e$$

### C. Flips Are for Gymnasts

Simplify the following expressions.

**a.** $1 + \dfrac{1}{1+1}$
  **b.** $1 + \dfrac{1}{1 + \dfrac{1}{1+1}}$

**c.** $1 + \dfrac{1}{1 + \dfrac{1}{1 + \dfrac{1}{1+1}}}$

See if you can discover a pattern and give the value of the following.

$$1 + \cfrac{1}{1 + \cfrac{1}{1 + \cfrac{1}{1 + \cfrac{1}{1 + \cfrac{1}{1 + \cfrac{1}{1 + \cfrac{1}{1 + \cfrac{1}{1+1}}}}}}}}$$

### 18-A  *X* MARKS THE SPOT

Work the following problem without doing a lot of arithmetic.

$$\frac{6831^2 - 6833^2}{(6833)(6832) - (6832)(6837)}$$

## 18-B  THE WHOLE IS GREATER THAN ITS PARTS

Unit fractions are fractions that have a numerator of 1 and a denominator of any whole number greater than 1. Can you find five *different* unit fractions whose sum is 1?

$$\frac{1}{a} + \frac{1}{b} + \frac{1}{c} + \frac{1}{d} + \frac{1}{e} = 1, \ a \neq b \neq c \neq d \neq e$$

### 18-C  FLIPS ARE FOR GYMNASTS

Simplify the following expressions,

**a.** $1 + \dfrac{1}{1+1}$

**b.** $1 + \dfrac{1}{1+\dfrac{1}{1+1}}$

**c.** $1 + \dfrac{1}{1+\dfrac{1}{1+\dfrac{1}{1+1}}}$

See if you can discover a pattern and give the value of the following.

$$1 + \cfrac{1}{1+\cfrac{1}{1+\cfrac{1}{1+\cfrac{1}{1+\cfrac{1}{1+\cfrac{1}{1+\cfrac{1}{1+\cfrac{1}{1+1}}}}}}}}$$

## 18-D  STAIR STEPS LEADING

Find the value of the following expression for $x = 1$ to 10.

$$\dfrac{\dfrac{1}{x} + \dfrac{1}{x^2} + \dfrac{1}{x^3}}{\dfrac{1}{x^4} + \dfrac{1}{x^5} + \dfrac{1}{x^6}}$$

# Problem Set 18
## ANSWERS AND SOLUTIONS

### A. *X* Marks the Spot

**Answer:** 1

**Solution:**

$$\frac{6831^2 - 6833^2}{(6833)(6832) - (6832)(6837)}$$

Let $x$ equal any one of the numbers. Express each of the other numbers in terms of $x$, and then simplify the result.

Let $x = 6833$

$$\frac{(x-2)^2 - x^2}{x(x-1) - (x-1)(x+4)} = \frac{x^2 - 4x + 4 - x^2}{x^2 - x - x^2 - 3x + 4}$$

$$= \frac{-4x + 4}{-4x + 4} = 1$$

### B. The Whole Is Greater Than Its Parts

**Answer:** Many different solutions

**Solution:**

One solution is dependent upon $\frac{1}{2} + \frac{1}{3} + \frac{1}{6} = 1$.

Rewrite $\frac{1}{3}$ as $\frac{3}{12}$, or $\frac{1}{12} + \frac{1}{6}$; then $\frac{1}{6} = \frac{3}{18} = \frac{1}{18} + \frac{1}{9}$;

and so $\frac{1}{2} + \frac{1}{12} + \frac{1}{6} + \frac{1}{18} + \frac{1}{9} = 1$.

### C. Flips Are for Gymnasts

**Answer:** $\dfrac{89}{55}$

**Solution:**

**a.** $1 + \dfrac{1}{1 + 1} = 1 + \dfrac{1}{2} = \dfrac{2 + 1}{2} = \dfrac{3}{2}$

**b.** $1 + \dfrac{1}{3/2} = 1 + \dfrac{2}{3} = \dfrac{3 + 2}{3} = \dfrac{5}{3}$

**c.** $1 + \dfrac{1}{5/3} = 1 + \dfrac{3}{5} = \dfrac{5 + 3}{5} = \dfrac{8}{5}$

It appears that the pattern, based on Fibonacci numbers, is

$$\frac{3}{2}, \frac{5}{3}, \frac{8}{5}, \frac{13}{8}, \frac{21}{13}, \frac{34}{21}, \frac{55}{34}, \frac{89}{55}$$

If you count the number of $1 +\ ^-$, this leads to a solution.

### D. Stair Steps Leading

**Answer:** 1, 8, 27, 64, 81, 125, 216, 343, 512, 729, 1000

**Solution:**

$$\frac{1/x + 1/x^2 + 1/x^3}{1/x^4 + 1/x^5 + 1/x^6}\ \text{simplifies to}$$

$$\frac{x^5 + x^4 + x^3}{x^2 + x + 1} = \frac{x^3(x^2 + x + 1)}{(x^2 + x + 1)} = x^3$$

This is an expression for generating the cubes.

### Problem Set 19
### PROBABILITY

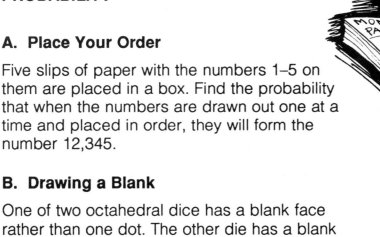

#### A. Place Your Order

Five slips of paper with the numbers 1–5 on them are placed in a box. Find the probability that when the numbers are drawn out one at a time and placed in order, they will form the number 12,345.

#### B. Drawing a Blank

One of two octahedral dice has a blank face rather than one dot. The other die has a blank face rather than three dots. Find the probability that a sum of nine appears when the dice are thrown. (Octahedral dice have eight faces with from one to eight dots on each of the faces.)

#### C. All's Fair in Love and Math

Decide whether the following dice game is a fair game. Two dice are thrown. If the sum of the dots is under seven, the player receives eight points. If the sum of the dots is seven or greater, the player loses six points. (*Hint:* How many points can a player expect to win or lose if 48 tosses are considered?)

## 19-A PLACE YOUR ORDER

Five slips of paper with the numbers 1–5 on them are placed in a box. Find the probability that when the numbers are drawn out one at a time and placed in order, they will form the number 12,345.

### 19-B  DRAWING A BLANK

One of two octahedral dice has a blank face rather than one dot. The other die has a blank face rather than three dots. Find the probability that a sum of nine appears when the dice are thrown. (Octahedral dice have eight faces with from one to eight dots on each of the faces.)

### 19-C  ALL'S FAIR IN LOVE AND MATH

Decide whether the following dice game is a fair game. Two dice are thrown. If the sum of the dots is under seven, the player receives eight points. If the sum of the dots is seven or greater, the player loses six points. (*Hint:* How many points can a player expect to win or lose if 48 tosses are considered?)

### 19-D  HIT OR MISS

In baseball, a batting average is the probability that a player will get a hit during his next at bat. Hank started a game with a 40% chance of getting a hit. After the game his percentage of hits was only 25%. What is the *fewest* number of at-bats he could have had in that game?

# Problem Set 19
## ANSWERS AND SOLUTIONS

### A. Place Your Order

**Answer:** $\dfrac{1}{120}$

**Solution:**

There are $5 \cdot 4 \cdot 3 \cdot 2 \cdot 1 = 120$ different five-digit numbers possible, only one of which gives a successful outcome.

$$P(E) = \frac{\text{successful outcomes}}{\text{possible outcomes}} = \frac{1}{120}$$

### B. Drawing a Blank

**Answer:** $\dfrac{3}{32}$

**Solution:**

There are $8 \cdot 8$, or 64, possible outcomes when two octahedral dice are thrown. If there were no blank faces, there would be eight possible sums of 9: (1, 8), (2, 7), (3, 6), (4, 5), (5, 4), (6, 3), (7, 2), (8, 1). Two of these, (1, 8) and (6, 3), must be thrown out to account for the blank faces. There are then only six successful outcomes.

$$P(9) = \frac{6}{64} = \frac{3}{32}$$

### C. All's Fair in Love and Math

**Answer:** It is not a fair game. There will be a loss of 8 points if 48 games are played.

**Solution:**

$$P(<7) = \frac{5}{12}; \; P(\geq 7) = \frac{7}{12}$$

In 48 games you will win $\dfrac{5}{12} \cdot 48 \cdot 8$, or 160, points. You will lose $\dfrac{7}{12} \cdot 48 \cdot 6$, or 168, points.

### D. Hit or Miss

**Answer:** 3

**Solution:**

Since the word *fewest* is emphasized, a batting average of 40%, or 0.4, is obtained by two hits in five at-bats. To have an average of 25% in the fewest number of bats, the only thing to change is the denominator of that ratio. Therefore,

$$\frac{2}{5 + x} = 25\% = \frac{1}{4}$$
$$5 + x = 8$$
$$x = 3$$

### Problem Set 20
### FRACTIONS

#### A. Dieters Can't Reduce Any Faster

Express as a fraction in lowest terms the value of the following product of 199 factors:

$$\left(1 - \frac{1}{2}\right)\left(1 - \frac{1}{3}\right)\left(1 - \frac{1}{4}\right)\cdots\left(1 - \frac{1}{n+1}\right)\cdots\left(1 - \frac{1}{200}\right)$$

#### B. Try an Alternate Route

Find both real values of $x$ that satisfy the equation

$$\left(\frac{3x-2}{2x-3}\right)^2 + \left(\frac{3x-2}{2x-3}\right) = 12$$

#### C. Enough for All

The new cinema wants to market a family-size portion of popcorn. The container will have a volume of 2535 in.$^3$ and will be an open square box 15 in. in depth made out of a square piece of cardboard by cutting out the corners and folding up the edges (see figure). Assuming you are not allowed to pile popcorn above the top of the container, find the length of a side of the original piece of cardboard.

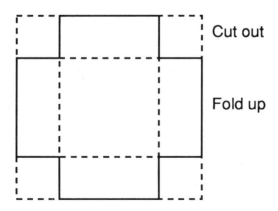

Cut out

Fold up

## 20-A DIETERS CAN'T REDUCE ANY FASTER

Express as a fraction in lowest terms the value of the following product of 199 factors:

$$\left(1 - \frac{1}{2}\right)\left(1 - \frac{1}{3}\right)\left(1 - \frac{1}{4}\right)\cdots\left(1 - \frac{1}{n+1}\right)\cdots\left(1 - \frac{1}{200}\right)$$

### 20-B   TRY AN ALTERNATE ROUTE

Find both real values of $x$ that satisfy the equation

$$\left(\frac{3x-2}{2x-3}\right)^2 + \left(\frac{3x-2}{2x-3}\right) = 12$$

## 20-C  ENOUGH FOR ALL

The new cinema wants to market a family-size portion of popcorn. The container will have a volume of 2535 in.³ and will be an open square box 15 in. in depth made out of a square piece of cardboard by cutting out the corners and folding up the edges (see figure). Assuming you are not allowed to pile popcorn above the top of the container, find the length of a side of the original piece of cardboard.

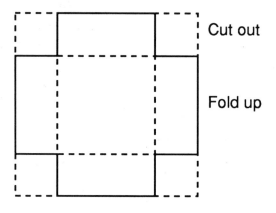

Cut out

Fold up

## 20-D  ARE WE PLANTING MORE SPINACH?

A rectangular garden is 9 ft longer than it is
wide. A second rectangular garden is
planned so that it will be 6 ft wider and twice
as long as the first garden. Find the area of
the first garden if the sum of the areas of both
gardens will be 528 ft².

# Problem Set 20
## ANSWERS AND SOLUTIONS

### A. Dieters Can't Reduce Any Faster

**Answer:** $\dfrac{1}{200}$

**Solution:**

Simplifying each part of the expression

$$\left(1 - \frac{1}{2}\right)\left(1 - \frac{1}{3}\right)\left(1 - \frac{1}{4}\right)\cdots\left(1 - \frac{1}{200}\right)$$

results in the product of the fractions $\dfrac{1}{2} \cdot \dfrac{2}{3} \cdot \dfrac{3}{4} \cdot \dfrac{4}{5} \cdots \dfrac{199}{200}$.

Simplifying this product leaves only factors of 1 in the numerator and 1s and 200 in the denominator.

### B. Try an Alternate Route

**Answer:** $\dfrac{14}{11}, \dfrac{7}{3}$

**Solution:**

$$\left(\frac{3x - 2}{2x - 3}\right)^2 + \left(\frac{3x - 2}{2x - 3}\right) = 12$$

can be solved more easily by letting

$y = \dfrac{3x - 2}{2x - 3}$ and then factoring the resulting equation. The

equation becomes $y^2 + y = 12$, or $y^2 + y - 12 = 0$. This equation yields $y = -4$ or $y = 3$. Solving for $x$:

$$\frac{3x - 2}{2x - 3} = -4 \quad \text{or} \quad \frac{3x - 2}{2x - 3} = 3$$

Solving each results in the desired solution.

### C. Enough for All

**Answer:** 43 x 43

**Solution:**

If the original square is $x$ by $x$ and the 15-in. squares are cut from the corners, a container of dimensions 15 by $x - 30$ by $x - 30$ will be formed.

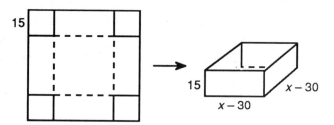

Since this volume is 2535, $15(x - 30)(x - 30) = 2535$. Solving gives $(x - 30)^2 = 169$, or

$$\begin{aligned} x - 30 &= \pm 13 \\ x &= 30 \pm 13 \\ x &= 43 \text{ or } 17 \end{aligned}$$

Since $17 - 30 < 0$, 17 can be discarded.

### D. Are We Planting More Spinach?

**Answer:** 112 ft$^2$

**Solution:**

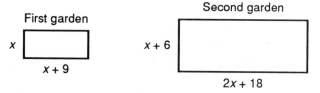

$$\begin{aligned} x(x + 9) + (x + 6)(2x + 18) &= 528 \\ x^2 + 9x + 2x^2 + 30x + 108 &= 528 \\ 3x^2 + 39x - 420 &= 0 \\ (3x + 60)(x - 7) &= 0 \\ x &= 7 \end{aligned}$$

The dimensions of the first garden are 7 x 16. The area is 112 ft$^2$.

## Problem Set 21
## INEQUALITIES

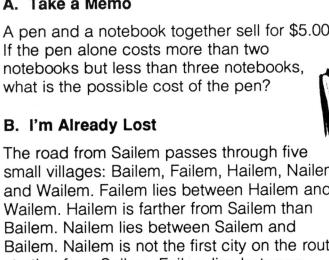

### A. Take a Memo

A pen and a notebook together sell for $5.00. If the pen alone costs more than two notebooks but less than three notebooks, what is the possible cost of the pen?

### B. I'm Already Lost

The road from Sailem passes through five small villages: Bailem, Failem, Hailem, Nailem, and Wailem. Failem lies between Hailem and Wailem. Hailem is farther from Sailem than Bailem. Nailem lies between Sailem and Bailem. Nailem is not the first city on the route starting from Sailem. Failem lies between Bailem and Nailem. Leaving Sailem, in what order do you pass through the five villages?

### C. Forced Separation

Given the digits 5, 5, 6, 6, 7, 7, 8, and 8, write an eight-digit number using these eight digits such that the
8s are separated by one digit
7s are separated by two digits
6s are separated by three digits, and
5s are separated by four digits.

### 21-A  TAKE A MEMO

A pen and a notebook together sell for $5.00.
If the pen alone costs more than two
notebooks but less than three notebooks,
what is the possible cost of the pen?

### 21-B I'M ALREADY LOST

The road from Sailem passes through five small villages: Bailem, Failem, Hailem, Nailem, and Wailem. Failem lies between Hailem and Wailem. Hailem is farther from Sailem than Bailem. Nailem lies between Sailem and Bailem. Nailem is not the first city on the route starting from Sailem. Failem lies between Bailem and Nailem. Leaving Sailem, in what order do you pass through the five villages?

## 21-C  FORCED SEPARATION

Given the digits 5, 5, 6, 6, 7, 7, 8, and 8, write an eight-digit number using these eight digits such that the
8s are separated by one digit
7s are separated by two digits
6s are separated by three digits, and
5s are separated by four digits.

### 21-D  FILL 'EM UP

A customer ordered 15 plants. Plants are placed in carriers that hold 4, 3, or 1 plant per carrier. In how many ways can this order be filled?

# Problem Set 21
## ANSWERS AND SOLUTIONS

### A. Take a Memo

**Answer:** The pen will cost between $3.33 and $3.75.

**Solution:**

If $p$ = price of a pen, then $5.00 − $p$ = price of a notebook.

2 notebooks < pen < 3 notebooks

$2(5 − p) < p < 3(5 − p)$

$10 − 2p < p < 15 − 3p$

$p > 10 − 2p$ and $p < 15 − 3p$

$3p > 10$ and $4p < 15$

$p > 3.33\frac{1}{3}$ and $p < 3.75$

### B. I'm Already Lost

**Answer:** Sailem, Wailem, Nailem, Failem, Bailem, Hailem

**Solution:**

The best technique for solving this problem involves paper shuffling. By placing each of the names on a separate piece of paper or 3- by 5-inch card, the order can be readily changed to satisfy each of the conditions of the problem.

### C. Forced Separation

**Answer:** One possible answer: 76,578,685

**Solution:**

The techniques of organized trial and error, again involving paper shuffling, can be used here. This answer is only one of several that will satisfy the given conditions.

### D. Fill 'Em Up

**Answer:** 15 ways

**Solution:**

Making a table is the best way to solve this problem.

| 4s | 3s | 1s |
|----|----|----|
| 0 | 0 | 15 |
| 0 | 1 | 12 |
| 0 | 2 | 9 |
| 0 | 3 | 6 |
| 0 | 4 | 3 |
| 0 | 5 | 0 |
| 1 | 0 | 11 |
| 1 | 1 | 8 |
| 1 | 2 | 5 |
| 1 | 3 | 2 |
| 2 | 0 | 7 |
| 2 | 1 | 4 |
| 2 | 2 | 1 |
| 3 | 0 | 3 |
| 3 | 1 | 0 |

Using triplets of numbers $(x, y, z)$, where $x$ = number of 4-plant carriers, $y$ = 3-plant carriers, and $z$ = 1-plant carriers, would also give the same solution.

## Problem Set 22
## COORDINATE SYSTEM

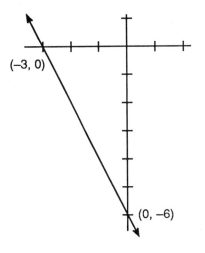

### A. I've Missed the Point

In order to save space, a small piece of graph paper has been used to show a line. Name the points on the line given only one of the coordinates:

**a.** (–20, ___)

**b.** (___, –100)

### B. What's My Rule?

Complete this sequence and find the *n*th term:

17, 25, 33, 41, 49, ___, ___, ___, . . . , ___
(nth term)

(Finding the *n*th term in a sequence is finding the general rule for all the terms in that sequence.)

### C. Don't Fence Me In

Find the area of a quadrilateral whose vertices have coordinates (–4, –6), (–3, 5), (4, 7), and (5, –9).

### 22-A  I'VE MISSED THE POINT

In order to save space, a small piece of graph paper has been used to show a line. Name the points on the line given only one of the coordinates:

**a.** (−20, ___)

**b.** (___, −100)

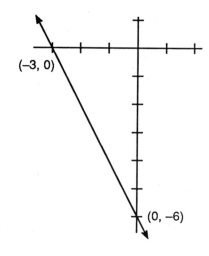

### 22-B  WHAT'S MY RULE?

Complete this sequence and find the *n*th term:

17, 25, 33, 41, 49, ___, ___, ___, . . . , ___
(nth term)

(Finding the *n*th term in a sequence is finding the general rule for all the terms in that sequence.)

### 22-C  DON'T FENCE ME IN

Find the area of a quadrilateral whose vertices have coordinates $(-4, -6)$, $(-3, 5)$, $(4, 7)$, and $(5, -9)$.

### 22-D ONE AT A TIME, PLEASE

A particle moves through the first quadrant as follows. During the first minute it moves from the origin (0, 0) to (1,0). Thereafter, it continues to move as shown in the figure, going back and forth between the positive x- and y-axes. The particle moves parallel to an axis and at a rate of speed of 1 unit per minute. What are the coordinates of the particle after 225 min?

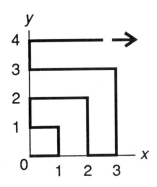

# Problem Set 22
## ANSWERS AND SOLUTIONS

### A. I've Missed the Point

**Answer: a.** (–20, 34); **b.** (47, –100)

**Solution:**

Using the general equation $y = mx + b$, the equation of the line becomes $y = -2x - 6$, since the slope ($m$) is –2 and the $y$-intercept ($b$) is –6. Substituting $x = -20$ into this equation results in $y = -2(-20) - 6$, or 34.

Substituting $y = -100$ results in

$$-100 = -2x - 6$$
$$-94 = -2x$$
$$x = 47$$

### B. What's My Rule?

**Answer:** 57, 65, 73, . . . , $8n + 9$

**Solution:**

Making a table with the counting numbers corresponding to successive terms in the sequence allows us to find an equation.

| $n$ | $f(n)$ |
|-----|--------|
| 1 | 17 |
| 2 | 25 |
| 3 | 33 |
| 4 | 41 |
| 5 | 49 |

Considering successive ordered pairs, (1, 17), (2, 25), (3, 33), and so on, we find that the slope between all points is 8, so that $f(n) = 8n + b$. Since $f(1) = 17$, we can find $b$ by solving the equation $17 = 8n + b$; $b = 9$. This gives the general equation $f(n) = 8n + 9$.

### C. Don't Fence Me In

**Answer:** 108

**Solution:**

The most understandable technique for solving is to enclose the quadrilateral in the smallest possible rectangle. Once this is accomplished, finding the area of the rectangle and subtracting the pieces that are in excess of the desired quadrilateral eventually results in the desired area.

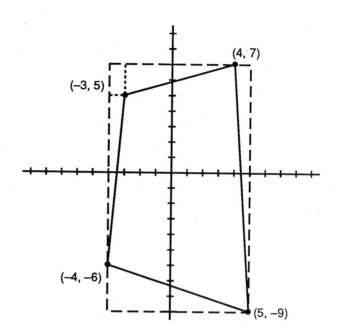

### D. One at a Time, Please

**Answer:** (15, 0)

**Solution:**

Examining a table to find the location after a number of minutes has passed reveals a pattern, as depicted in the following table.

| Minutes | Location |
|---------|----------|
| 1 | (1, 0) |
| 4 | (0, 2) |
| 9 | (3, 0) |
| 16 | (0, 4) |
| 25 | (5, 0) |

Remarkably, the point is always on an axis when the number of minutes that has elapsed is a perfect square. Not only is it on the axis, the coordinates are related to the square root of the elapsed time. The pattern reveals that for an odd perfect square, the particle is on the $x$-axis, whereas it is on the $y$-axis for an even perfect square. Since 225 is odd, the particle will be located at $(\sqrt{225}, 0)$, or (15, 0).

### Problem Set 23
### COORDINATE SYSTEM

#### A. What's the Plot?

If a point starts at (0, 0) on the grid given and moves as illustrated, find the coordinates of its final position after 100 moves.

$(0, 0) \rightarrow (1, -1) \rightarrow (3, 1) \rightarrow (0, 4) \rightarrow (-4, 0) \rightarrow \ldots$

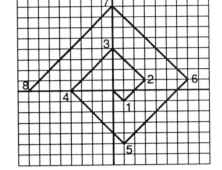

#### B. Card Tricks

How many combinations of 8¢ and 15¢ postcards can be purchased by spending exactly $4.80? List each combination.

#### C. Fill It Up!

Complete the following table for the missing entries and try to express a general rule.

| $x$ | 1 | 2 | 3 | 4 | 5 | 6 | 7 | $\cdots$ | 100 | $\cdots$ | $x$ |
|-----|---|---|---|----|----|---|---|----------|-----|----------|-----|
| $y$ | 1 | 3 | 6 | 10 | 15 | — | — | $\cdots$ | — | $\cdots$ | $y =$ __ $x +$ __ |

### 23-A  WHAT'S THE PLOT?

If a point starts at (0, 0) on the grid given and
moves as illustrated, find the coordinates of
its final position after 100 moves.

$(0, 0) \rightarrow (1, -1) \rightarrow (3, 1) \rightarrow (0, 4) \rightarrow (-4, 0) \rightarrow \ldots$

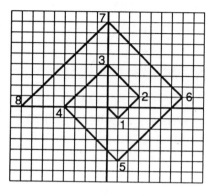

## 23-B CARD TRICKS

How many combinations of 8¢ and 15¢
postcards can be purchased by spending
exactly $4.80? List each combination.

## 23-C  FILL IT UP!

Complete the following table for the missing entries and try to express a
general rule.

| x | 1 | 2 | 3 | 4 | 5 | 6 | 7 | $\cdots$ | 100 | $\cdots$ | x |
|---|---|---|---|---|---|---|---|---|---|---|---|
| y | 1 | 3 | 6 | 10 | 15 | — | — | $\cdots$ | — | $\cdots$ | $y = \underline{\quad} x + \underline{\quad}$ |

### 23-D NO ENGLISH, PLEASE

On graph paper mark the lines $y = 6$, $x = 12$, and both axes. The rectangle formed represents a pool table. A "pool rule" states that a ball traveling along a line with slope $m$ and striking the side of a table will bounce back along a line with slope $-m$. (*Remember:* In graph-paper pool, the path of the ball must hit at exactly the coordinates of the pocket.)

**a.** A ball starts at (8, 3) with slope 2 toward the $x$-axis. Where does it strike the $x$-axis?

**b.** Assume the pockets are located at the vertices of the rectangle and at the midpoints of the longest sides. If the ball from part a has a continuous motion, will it eventually go into one of the six pockets? If so, what coordinates does the pocket have?

**c.** If the ball is located at (8, 3) and you want to shoot the ball into the pocket at (0, 6) by rebounding it off only one side of the table, what would be the slope of the line that represents your shot?

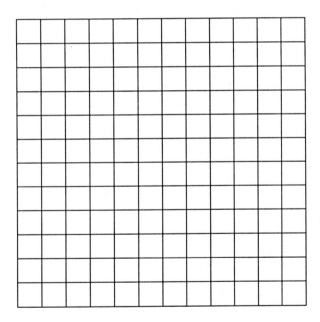

# Problem Set 23
## ANSWERS AND SOLUTIONS

### A. What's the Plot?

**Answer:** (−100, 0)

**Solution:**

We need to consider only where the point is located after every fourth move, since the point is always located on the negative side of the x-axis. After four moves, it will be at (− 4, 0); after eight moves, at (− 8, 0); after 100 moves, at (−100, 0).

### B. Card Tricks

**Answer:** (0, 32), (15, 24), (30, 16), (45, 8), (60, 0), where (x, y) represents (8¢ cards, 15¢ cards)

**Solution:**

Since 480 is a multiple of both 8 and 15, two pairs, (0,32) and (60, 0), can be found easily. Using these two points and the slope-intercept form of a line, the equation is $y = \dfrac{-8}{15} x + 32$. Since solutions must be positive integers, using multiples of 15 for x reveals the other solutions.

### C. Fill It Up!

**Answer:** 21, 28, . . ., 5050: $y = \dfrac{x(x+1)}{2}$, or $\dfrac{1}{2}x^2 + \dfrac{1}{2}x$

**Solution:**

Examining only y values shows that the equation used to describe this function is not linear. There are several techniques for solving quadratic functions, but Gauss's technique is good. The series 1, 3, 6, 10, 15, . . . represents the sum of consecutive integers, i.e., 1 = 1, 1 + 2 = 3, 1 + 2 + 3 = 6, 1 + 2 + 3 + 4 = 10, and so on. To find the value when x = 100, the sum 1 + 2 + 3 + 4 + . . . +100 must be found. Gauss's formula is $\dfrac{n(n+1)}{2}$, where n is the number of consecutive integers. To find the rule desired, substitute x into the formula in place of n .

### D. No English, Please

**Answer:** See Solution.

**Solution:**

**a.** $(6\dfrac{1}{2}, 0)$

**b.** The ball will never go into a pocket. A sketch of the table will show this.

**c.** To achieve the desired result, the ball must be rebounded off either the x-axis or the line x = 12. Using reflections, hitting toward the x-axis would result in the ball going straight into an imaginary pocket at (0, −6). The slope between (8, 3) and (0, −6) is $\dfrac{9}{8}$. This slope gives one possible solution.

Rebounding off the line x = 12, hitting toward (24, 6) would result in the ball rebounding into (0, 6). The slope between (24, 6) and (8, 3) is $\dfrac{3}{16}$, the slope of the other possible path.

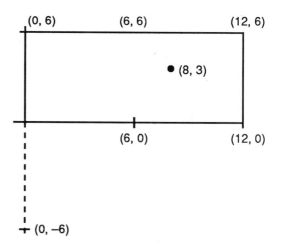

## Problem Set 24
## SYSTEMS OF EQUATIONS

### A. Keep Them Rolling

When Amy was asked to count the number of tricycles and bicycles in her mother's bicycle shop, she got bored. Rather than just counting the vehicles, she decided to count the number of pedals and the number of wheels. She counted 132 wheels and 112 pedals. How many bicycles and how many tricycles did her mother have in her shop?

### B. Up, Up, and Away

Nicholas, who is always in a hurry, walks up a moving escalator in a department store. He takes 2 steps per second and reaches the top after taking 32 steps. When he is tired, he walks up the same escalator and takes only 1 step per second, reaching the top after 20 steps. How many steps are there in the escalator and what is the speed of the escalator in steps per second?

### C. Once Around the Block

Two identical blocks of wood are placed as shown in Figure 1, one on top of the table and the other at its base. Length *a* is found to be 32 in. After the blocks are rearranged as shown in Figure 2, length *b* is found to be 28 in. What is the height of the table?

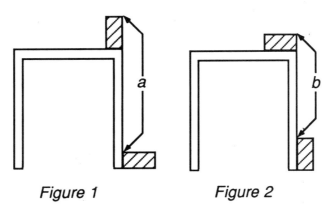

Figure 1          Figure 2

### 24-A  KEEP THEM ROLLING

When Amy was asked to count the number of tricycles and bicycles in her mother's bicycle shop, she got bored. Rather than just counting the vehicles, she decided to count the number of pedals and the number of wheels. She counted 132 wheels and 112 pedals. How many bicycles and how many tricycles did her mother have in her shop?

### 24-B  UP, UP, AND AWAY

Nicholas, who is always in a hurry, walks up a moving escalator in a department store. He takes 2 steps per second and reaches the top after taking 32 steps. When he is tired, he walks up the same escalator and takes only 1 step per second, reaching the top after 20 steps. How many steps are there in the escalator and what is the speed of the escalator in steps per second?

### 24-C ONCE AROUND THE BLOCK

Two identical blocks of wood are placed as shown in Figure 1, one on top of the table and the other at its base. Length *a* is found to be 32 in. After the blocks are rearranged as shown in Figure 2, length *b* is found to be 28 in. What is the height of the table?

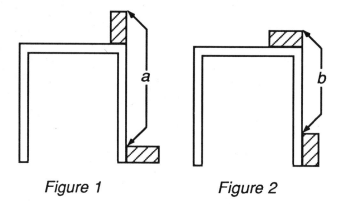

Figure 1          Figure 2

## 24-D  THE WHOLE BUNCH

Julie harvested three watermelons from her garden. The largest weighed as much as the other two, the smallest weighed 1 lb less than one-fourth the other two together, and the whole bunch weighed 24 lb. What was the weight of each watermelon?

# Problem Set 24
## ANSWERS AND SOLUTIONS

### A. Keep Them Rolling

**Answer:** 36 bicycles and 20 tricycles

**Solution:**
Since there are two pedals per vehicle, the equation for pedals is $2x + 2y = 112$. Three wheels for a tricycle and two for a bicycle gives $3x + 2y = 132$.

### B. Up, Up, and Away

**Answer:** 80 steps; 3 steps per second

**Solution:**
Let $y =$ number of steps
$\quad\quad x =$ speed in steps per second

When Nicholas takes 2 steps per second and reaches the top after taking 32 steps, he takes 16 seconds to reach the top; $y = 16x + 32$ represents the number of steps. When Nicholas takes 1 step per second, it takes him 20 seconds to reach the top. $y = 20x + 20$ represents the number of steps.

$$20x + 20 = 16x + 32$$
$$4x = 12$$
$$x = 3$$
$$y = 16(3) + 32 = 80$$

### C. Once Around the Block

**Answer:** 30 in.

**Solution:**
Let the block of wood be $x$ by $y$ and the height be $h$.

*Figure 1* $\quad h = a + x - y$ $\quad\quad$ *Figure 2* $\quad h = b + y - x$
$\quad\quad\quad\quad\quad h = 32 + x - y$ $\quad\quad\quad\quad\quad\quad\quad h = 28 + y - x$

Adding the equations gives $2h = 60$, or $h = 30$.

### D. The Whole Bunch

**Answer:** 12, 8, 4

**Solution:**
Since the combined weight is 24 and the heaviest watermelon weighs the same as the sum of the other two, the equations needed refer only to the two smallest watermelons.

$$x + y = 12$$
$$x = \frac{1}{4}(y + 12) - 1, \text{ or } x = \frac{1}{4}y + 2$$

Solving yields $x = 4$ and $y = 8$.

## Problem Set 25
## SYSTEMS OF EQUATIONS

### A. Help Wanted

Arbegla and Eno can complete a job in 18 min working together. Working alone, Eno would require 15 min more than Arbegla to complete the job. How long does it take Eno to do the entire job by himself?

### B. Send Me in, Coach

If $x = -y - z + 3$, $2x + y - z = -6$, and $3x - y + z = 11$, find the values for $x$, $y$, and $z$ that will make all three statements true.

### C. Rapid Transit

Reed and his brother Ryan can put 9 mi between them in 20 min when starting from the same point and skating at top speed in opposite directions. It takes the same time for Reed to pull a mile ahead of Ryan when they're skating in the same direction (again starting from the same point). What is each one's top speed?

## 25-A  HELP WANTED

Arbegla and Eno can complete a job in
18 min working together. Working alone, Eno
would require 15 min more than Arbegla to
complete the job. How long does it take Eno
to do the entire job by himself?

### 25-B SEND ME IN, COACH

If $x = -y - z + 3$, $2x + y - z = -6$, and
$3x - y + z = 11$, find the values for $x$, $y$, and $z$
that will make all three statements true.

## 25-C RAPID TRANSIT

Reed and his brother Ryan can put 9 mi
between them in 20 min when starting from
the same point and skating at top speed in
opposite directions. It takes the same time for
Reed to pull a mile ahead of Ryan when
they're skating in the same direction (again
starting from the same point). What is each
one's top speed?

## 25-D  DON'T BLOCK MY SUN

A solar-powered car is being test-driven. The vehicle is driven at 30 mph under solar power and 40 mph under regular power. The trip to the nearest town takes 45 min using both solar and regular power, whereas the return trip takes 50 min using only solar power. On the trip to the town, find the distance driven using solar power and the distance driven using regular power.

# Problem Set 25
## ANSWERS AND SOLUTIONS

### A. Help Wanted

**Answer:** 45 min

**Solution:**

Solving the equations $A = E + 15$ and $\dfrac{18}{A} + \dfrac{18}{E} = 1$ yields the solution. Using substitution and clearing fractions yields the quadratic $E^2 - 21E - 270 = 0$.
Solving by factoring gives $E = 30$ and $A = 30 + 15$, or 45.

### B. Send Me in, Coach

**Answer:** $x = 1$, $y = -3$, $z = 5$

**Solution:**

This problem is set up to be turned into a system with two equations and two variables by using substitution. Since $x = -y - z + 3$, $2x + y - z = -6$ becomes $2(-y - z + 3) + y - z = -6$ and $3x - y + z = 11$ becomes $3(-y - z + 3) - y + z = 11$. Simplifying each gives the system $y + 3z = 12$ and $-4y - 2z = 2$.

### C. Rapid Transit

**Answer:** 15 mph and 12 mph

**Solution:**

Let $x$ = Reed's speed and $y$ = Ryan's speed.

$\dfrac{1}{3}x + \dfrac{1}{3}y = 9$   opposite direction

$\dfrac{1}{3}x = \dfrac{1}{3}y + 1$   same direction

$\dfrac{2}{3}x = 10$

$x = 15$

### D. Don't Block My Sun

**Answer:** 15 mi using solar power, 10 mi using regular power

**Solution:**

Let $x$ = distance using solar power and $y$ = distance using regular power. Using $d = rt$ yields the system of equations needed to solve this problem.

The equations are $\dfrac{x}{30} + \dfrac{y}{40} = \dfrac{3}{4}$ and $\dfrac{x + y}{30} = \dfrac{5}{6}$.

### Problem Set 26
### MISCELLANY

### A. Role Reversal

Four times the tens digit of a two-digit number increased by the units digit is 18. If the digits are reversed, the new number is 9 less than twice the original number. Find the original number.

### B. Going in Circles

Draw each of the following graphs on the same set of axes and then complete the shading so that your graph represents a familiar object: $(x + 4)^2 + y^2 = 81$; $(x - 2)^2 + (y - 1)^2 = 1$; $(x - 2)^2 + y^2 = 9$; and $(x - 2)^2 + (y + 1)^2 = 1$. Do some research on conic sections before you graph these.

### C. Where There's Smoke

A fire on a line with slope $\frac{2}{3}$ was spotted from a fire tower located at $(-1, 0)$. The same fire was spotted on a line with slope $-\frac{2}{3}$ from a second fire tower located at $(14, -2)$. What are the coordinates of the fire?

## 26-A  ROLE REVERSAL

Four times the tens digit of a two-digit number increased by the units digit is 18. If the digits are reversed, the new number is 9 less than twice the original number. Find the original number.

### 26-B  GOING IN CIRCLES

Draw each of the following graphs on the
same set of axes and then complete the
shading so that your graph represents a
familiar object: $(x + 4)^2 + y^2 = 81$;
$(x - 2)^2 + (y - 1)^2 = 1$; $(x - 2)^2 + y^2 = 9$;
and $(x - 2)^2 + (y + 1)^2 = 1$. Do some research
on conic sections before you graph these.

### 26-C  WHERE THERE'S SMOKE

A fire on a line with slope $\frac{2}{3}$ was spotted from a fire tower located at $(-1, 0)$. The same fire was spotted on a line with slope $-\frac{2}{3}$ from a second fire tower located at $(14, -2)$. What are the coordinates of the fire?

### 26-D  ENTRANCE EXAM

At Math Tech High, school starts between 8:00 AM and 9:00 AM when the hands of a clock are together. Classes are over between 2:00 PM and 3:00 PM when the hands are exactly 180° apart. How long does a student go to school at Math Tech?

# Problem Set 26
## ANSWERS AND SOLUTIONS

### A. Role Reversal

**Answer:** 36

**Solution:**

Let $t$ = tens digit and $u$ = units digit

$10t + u$ = original number

$10u + t$ = new number

$4t + u = 18$

$2(10t + u) = 10u + t - 9$

Solving this system gives $t = 3$ and $u = 6$.

### B. Going in Circles

**Answer:** The graph shows an eight ball.

**Solution:**

Each equation describes a circle, using $(x - h)^2 + (y - k)^2 = r^2$ where $(h, k)$ is the center and $r$ is the radius.

### C. Where There's Smoke

**Answer:** The fire is located at (5, 4).

**Solution:**

The fire is located at the intersection of the two lines, one passing through $(-1, 0)$ with slope $\frac{2}{3}$ and the other passing through $(14, -2)$ with slope $-\frac{2}{3}$. The two equations of these lines are $2x - 3y = -2$ and $2x + 3y = 22$, respectively. Solving these simultaneously leads to the answer.

### D. Entrance Exam

**Answer:** 6 h

**Solution:**

If $x$ = distance the minute hand travels and $y$ = distance the hour hand travels, the equations $x = 12y$ and $x = y + 40$ are obtained, since the minute hand must travel 12 times further and the hour hand has a 40-unit start. Solving yields $y = 3\frac{7}{11}$, $x = 43\frac{7}{11}$. Therefore, the starting time is $8:43\frac{7}{11}$. To be 180° apart, the hands must have a 30-unit difference between them, so $x = y + 10 + 30$ and $x = 12y$. Solving again yields $y = 3\frac{7}{11}$; therefore, the finishing time is $2:43\frac{7}{11}$ PM.

## Problem Set 27
## PERFECT SQUARES

### A. Root for the Underdog

The digital root of a number is found by adding all the digits of the number and of that result, and so on until a single digit is obtained. The digital root of 759 is 3 because $7 + 5 + 9 = 21$ and $2 + 1 = 3$. The digital root of 813,520 is 1 because $8 + 1 + 3 + 5 + 2 + 0 = 19$, $1 + 9 = 10$, and $1 + 0 = 1$. If a number is the square of a positive integer, find the numbers that are possible digital roots.

### B. Penned In

Three squares with areas of 64, 225, and 289 square units are arranged so that when vertices coincide a triangle is formed. Find the area of that triangle.

### C. Got You Covered

Three squares with areas of 17, 25, and 26 square units are arranged as shown in the diagram. Lines are drawn to make the figure a convex polygon. Find the area of the polygon. (*Hint:* Try drawing a similar figure on graph paper and then count the squares enclosed.)

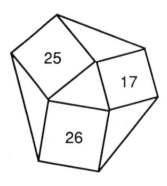

## 27-A ROOT FOR THE UNDERDOG

The digital root of a number is found by adding all the digits of the number and of that result, and so on until a single digit is obtained. The digital root of 759 is 3 because $7 + 5 + 9 = 21$ and $2 + 1 = 3$. The digital root of 813,520 is 1 because $8 + 1 + 3 + 5 + 2 + 0 = 19$, $1 + 9 = 10$, and $1 + 0 = 1$. If a number is the square of a positive integer, find the numbers that are possible digital roots.

## 27-B  PENNED IN

Three squares with areas of 64, 225, and 289
square units are arranged so that when
vertices coincide a triangle is formed. Find the
area of that triangle.

## 27-C  GOT YOU COVERED

Three squares with areas of 17, 25, and 26
square units are arranged as shown in the
diagram. Lines are drawn to make the figure a
convex polygon. Find the area of the polygon.
(*Hint:* Try drawing a similar figure on graph
paper and then count the squares enclosed.)

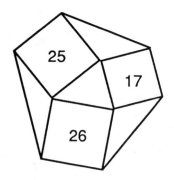

### 27-D  WHAT A MESS

During a recent election to determine the president of a major company, the votes were counted in secrecy. It was noted that each of the candidates received more than 100,000 votes and that the number of votes received by the winner was a perfect square. Unfortunately, before the results could be read at the board meeting, someone spilled some coffee. Can you examine this salvaged piece of paper and determine the winner?

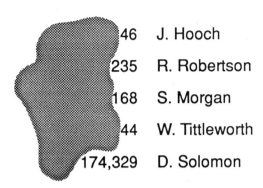

46      J. Hooch

235     R. Robertson

168     S. Morgan

44      W. Tittleworth

174,329 D. Solomon

# Problem Set 27
## ANSWERS AND SOLUTIONS

### A. Root for the Underdog

**Answer:** 1, 4, 7, 9

**Solution:**

A chart reveals that only four numbers are possible. Since the question works only with perfect squares, numbers in the sequence 1, 4, 9, 16, 25, 36, and so on are examined.

| $n^2$ | Digital root | $n^2$ | Digital root |
|---|---|---|---|
| 1 | 1 | 100 | 1 |
| 4 | 4 | 121 | 4 |
| 9 | 9 | 144 | 9 |
| 16 | 7 | 169 → 16 | 7 |
| 25 | 7 | 196 → 16 | 7 |
| 36 | 9 | 225 | 7 |
| 49 → 13 | 4 | 256 → 13 | 4 |
| 64 → 10 | 1 | 289 → 19 → 10 | 1 |
| 81 | 9 | 324 | 9 |

### B. Penned in

**Answer:** 60

**Solution:**

Since $64 + 225 = 289$, the triangle enclosed is a right triangle with legs 8 and 15 and hypotenuse 17. The area therefore is $\frac{1}{2} \cdot 8 \cdot 15$, or 60.

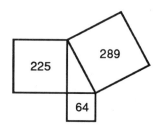

### C. Got You Covered

**Answer:** 106 square units

**Solution:**

The key to this problem involves drawing a similar figure on graph paper. Squares with areas of 25, 17, and 26 can be drawn by considering right triangles $3^2 + 4^2 = 25$, $4^2 + 1^2 = 17$, and $5^2 + 1^2 = 26$. The rectangle that encloses the desired area has dimensions 12 x 13, or 156 square units.

Subtracting the eight identified areas (see Roman numerals) leaves the desired area:

$$156 - (3 + 10\frac{1}{2} + 6 + 9 + 2 + 2\frac{1}{2} + 15 + 2)$$

$$= 156 - (50) = 106$$

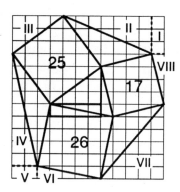

### D. What a Mess

**Answer:** W. Tittleworth

**Solution:**

Since the number of votes the winner received is a perfect square, D. Solomon can be eliminated, since 174, 329 is not a perfect square. A perfect square must end in 0, 1, 4, 5, 6, or 9, eliminating S. Morgan. Considering the possibilities for $r^2$:

| | |
|---|---|
| $0^2 = 0 = 00$ | $5^2 = 25$ |
| $1^2 = 1 = 01$ | $6^2 = 36$ |
| $2^2 = 4 = 04$ | $7^2 = 49$ |
| $3^2 = 9 = 09$ | $8^2 = 64$ |
| $4^2 = 16 = 16$ | $9^2 = 81$ |

R. Robertson can be eliminated because a perfect square ending in 5 must have a 2 for the next-to-the-last digit.
J. Hooch can be eliminated, since a perfect square ending in 6 must have an odd digit as the next-to-the-last digit.

## Problem Set 28
## RADICALS

### A. Stay on the Path

A point $P$ starts at (0, 0) and moves consecutively in the following way: Move 1 is 1 unit to the right, move 2 is 2 up, move 3 is 3 left, move 4 is 4 down, move 5 is 5 right, and so on. Find the coordinates of $P$ and the distance ($d$) the point is from its original starting point after 50 moves.

### B. Does Not Compute

The sum of two numbers is 12, and their product is 24. Find the sum of the reciprocals of the two numbers.

### C. Triple-Decker

If $ab = 15$, $ac = 36$, and $bc = 60$, find $abc$.

### 28-A  STAY ON THE PATH

A point *P* starts at (0, 0) and moves consecutively in the following way: Move 1 is 1 unit to the right, move 2 is 2 up, move 3 is 3 left, move 4 is 4 down, move 5 is 5 right, and so on. Find the coordinates of *P* and the distance (*d*) the point is from its original starting point after 50 moves.

## 28-B  DOES NOT COMPUTE

The sum of two numbers is 12, and their product is 24. Find the sum of the reciprocals of the two numbers.

### 28-C  TRIPLE-DECKER

If $ab = 15$, $ac = 36$, and $bc = 60$, find $abc$.

## 28-D  MAKE IT A TWOSOME

The sum of two numbers is 10, and the product of the same two numbers is 20. Find the sum of the squares of the two numbers.

# Problem Set 28
## ANSWERS AND SOLUTIONS

### A. Stay on the Path

**Answer:** $P = (25, 26)$; $d = \sqrt{1301}$

**Solution:**
Listing coordinates after each move gives the following sequence of ordered pairs.

| Moves | Location |
|-------|----------|
| 1 | (1, 0) |
| 2 | (1, 2) |
| 3 | (−2, 2) |
| 4 | (−2, −2) |
| 5 | (3, −2) |
| 6 | (3, 4) |
| 7 | (−4, 4) |
| 8 | (−4, −4) |
| 9 | (5, −4) |
| 10 | (5, 6) |

Every fourth move reveals a pattern. Since $50 + 4 = 12$ with a remainder of 2, we are concerned only with moves in the sequence 2, 6, 10, 14, . . . , 50. Moves in this sequence can be expressed by the following relation. After $n$ moves the point will be located at $(\frac{n}{2}, \frac{n}{2} + 1)$. Therefore, after 50 moves the coordinates of the point will be $(\frac{50}{2}, \frac{50}{2} + 1)$, or (25, 26).

$$d = \sqrt{(25 - 0)^2 + (26 - 0)^2}$$

### B. Does Not Compute

**Answer:** $\dfrac{1}{2}$

**Solution:**
Although this problem can be solved using the system of equations $x + y = 12$ and $x \cdot y = 24$, a more surprising solution comes from adding the reciprocals of the two numbers. The reciprocals of $x$ and $y$ are $\frac{1}{x}$ and $\frac{1}{y}$, so the sum is $\frac{1}{x} + \frac{1}{y}$, or $\frac{y + x}{xy}$. Since both $x + y$ and $x \cdot y$ are known, the sum $\frac{1}{x} + \frac{1}{y}$ can be given as $\frac{12}{24}$, or $\frac{1}{2}$.

### C. Triple-Decker

**Answer:** ±180

**Solution:**
This problem can be solved using successive substitution to find exact values for $a$, $b$, and $c$. Since only the product $abc$ is desired, an alternate solution can be used. Since $ab = 15$, $ac = 36$, and $bc = 60$, multiplying the three equations together results in $a^2b^2c^2 = 15 \cdot 36 \cdot 60$. Therefore, $abc = \pm\sqrt{15 \cdot 36 \cdot 60}$, or $\pm(15 \cdot 6 \cdot 2)$. If $a$, $b$, $c > 0$, then $abc = 180$. If $a$, $b$, $c < 0$, then $abc = -180$.

### D. Make It a Twosome

**Answer:** 60

**Solution:**
This problem can be solved using the system of equations $x + y = 10$ and $x \cdot y = 20$. Squaring $x + y = 10$ gives $x^2 + 2xy + y^2 = 100$. Since $xy = 20$, $2xy = 40$. Substitution leads to $x^2 + 40 + y^2 = 100$, or $x^2 + y^2 = 60$, the desired result.

## Problem Set 29
## RADICALS

### A. Root It Out

Find $x$ if $\sqrt[3]{x\sqrt{x}} = 9$.

### B. Is That a Fact?

$\sqrt{x} + \sqrt{y} = 17$ and $x - y = 51$. Find all pairs $(x, y)$ that make each statement true.

### C. Ups and Downs

If $a \uparrow b$ means $a^b$ and $a \downarrow b$ means $\sqrt[b]{a}$, find the value of $[(4 \uparrow 4) \downarrow 2] \uparrow 3$.

## 29-A  ROOT IT OUT

Find $x$ if $\sqrt[3]{x\sqrt{x}} = 9$.

## 29-B  IS THAT A FACT?

$\sqrt{x} + \sqrt{y} = 17$ and $x - y = 51$. Find all pairs $(x, y)$ that make each statement true.

### 29-C  UPS AND DOWNS

If $a \uparrow b$ means $a^b$ and $a \downarrow b$ means $\sqrt[b]{a}$, find the value of $[(4 \uparrow 4) \downarrow 2] \uparrow 3$.

## 29-D  EXACTLY RIGHT

Find all values of $x$ that satisfy

$$4 - \frac{3}{x} = \sqrt{4 - \frac{3}{x}}.$$

# Problem Set 29
## ANSWERS AND SOLUTIONS

### A. Root It Out

**Answer:** 81

**Solution:**

The solution involves cubing and then squaring both sides of the equation to eliminate all the radical signs. Cubing

$\sqrt[3]{x\sqrt{x}} = 9$ gives $x\sqrt{x} = 9^3$. Squaring $x\sqrt{x} = 9^3$ gives $x^2 \cdot x = 9^6$. Solving $x^3 = 9^6$ gives $x = 9^2$ or 81.

### B. Is That a Fact?

**Answer:** The only pair is $x = 100$, $y = 49$.

**Solution:**

Since $x = \sqrt{x} \cdot \sqrt{x}$ and $y = \sqrt{y} \cdot \sqrt{y}$, $x - y$ can be factored as $(\sqrt{x} + \sqrt{y})(\sqrt{x} - \sqrt{y})$. Since $\sqrt{x} + \sqrt{y} = 17$, it follows that $\sqrt{x} - \sqrt{y} = 3$, since $(\sqrt{x} + \sqrt{y})(\sqrt{x} - \sqrt{y}) = 51$. Solving $\sqrt{x} + \sqrt{y} = 17$ and $\sqrt{x} - \sqrt{y} = 3$ yields

$$2\sqrt{x} = 20$$
$$\sqrt{x} = 10$$
$$x = 100$$

Since $x - y = 51$, $100 - y = 51$ and $y = 49$.

### C. Ups and Downs

**Answer:** 4096

**Solution:**

Rewriting $[(4 \uparrow 4) \downarrow 2] \uparrow 3$ using standard notation results in $\left[\sqrt{4^4}\right]^3$. Simplifying $\sqrt{4^4}$ results in $4^2$, so the solution is $\left[4^2\right]^3$, or $4^6 = 4096$.

### D. Exactly Right

**Answer:** $x = 1$ or $x = \dfrac{3}{4}$

**Solution:**

In the real-number system, the only numbers whose square roots are the same as the number are 1 and 0. Therefore $4 - \dfrac{3}{x} = 1$ or $4 - \dfrac{3}{x} = 0$. Solving each of these leads to the solutions 1 and $\dfrac{3}{4}$. An alternate solution involves squaring both sides of the equation, resulting in $16 - \dfrac{24}{x} + \dfrac{9}{x^2} = 4 - \dfrac{3}{x}$. Clearing of fractions and then regrouping results in $12x^2 - 21x + 9 = 0$. Factoring gives $3(4x - 3)(x - 1) = 0$, which results in $x = 1$ or $x = \dfrac{3}{4}$.

### Problem Set 30
### RADICALS

#### A. Check This Out

Find all the values of $x$ such that
$\dfrac{4}{x} + \dfrac{x}{4} = \dfrac{5}{x} + \dfrac{x}{5}$. Show a check of
your answers.

#### B. Infinitely Yours

Find the *exact* value of

$$\sqrt{12 + \sqrt{12 + \sqrt{12 + \cdots}}}.$$

(*Hint:* If $S = \sqrt{12 + \sqrt{12 + \sqrt{12 + \cdots}}}$,
think about $S^2$.)

#### C. Where Do I Start?

Find the *exact* value of $\sqrt{13 + \sqrt{2} + \dfrac{7}{3 + \sqrt{2}}}$.

## 30-A CHECK THIS OUT

Find all the values of $x$ such that

$\dfrac{4}{x} + \dfrac{x}{4} = \dfrac{5}{x} + \dfrac{x}{5}$. Show a check of

your answers.

### 30-B   INFINITELY YOURS

Find the *exact* value of

$$\sqrt{12 + \sqrt{12 + \sqrt{12 + \cdots}}}.$$

(*Hint:* If $S = \sqrt{12 + \sqrt{12 + \sqrt{12 + \cdots}}}$,
think about $S^2$.)

### 30-C  WHERE DO I START?

Find the *exact* value of $\sqrt{13 + \sqrt{2} + \dfrac{7}{3 + \sqrt{2}}}$.

### 30-D  PRIME-TIME VIEWING

Find the smallest set of different primes, *A*, *B*, *C*, and D, so that each of the following statements is true:

$B = \sqrt{A - 2} + 2$

$C = \sqrt{B - 2} + 2$

$D = \sqrt{C - 2} + 2$

# Problem Set 30
## ANSWERS AND SOLUTIONS

### A. Check This Out

**Answer:** $\pm 2\sqrt{5}$

**Solution:**

If $\dfrac{4}{x} + \dfrac{x}{4} = \dfrac{5}{x} + \dfrac{x}{5}$, then clearing of fractions results in the equations $80 + 5x^2 = 100 + 4x^2$. Solving gives $x^2 = 20$, or $\pm\sqrt{20} = \pm 2\sqrt{5}$. This problem is more interesting if you consider the case of all consecutive integers, that is,

$$\frac{a}{x} + \frac{x}{a} = \frac{a+1}{x} + \frac{x}{a+1}.$$

After clearing of fractions, this equation yields the following successive results.

$$\frac{a^2 + x^2}{ax} = \frac{a^2 + 2a + 1 + x^2}{x(a+1)}$$

$$(a^2 + x^2)(a+1) = a(a^2 + 2a + 1 + x^2)$$

$$a^3 + a^2 + ax^2 + x^2 = a^3 + 2a^2 + a + ax^2$$

$$x^2 = a^2 + a$$

$$x = \pm\sqrt{a^2 + a}$$

$$= \pm\sqrt{a(a+1)}$$

### B. Infinitely Yours

**Answer:** 4

**Solution:**

If $S = \sqrt{12 + \sqrt{12 + \sqrt{12 + \cdots}}}$,

then $S^2 = 12 + \sqrt{12 + \sqrt{12 + \sqrt{12 + \cdots}}}$. Substituting results in the equation $S^2 = 12 + S$. Solving $S^2 = 12 + S$ results in $S = 4$ or $S = -3$. Since square root is defined to be positive, $-3$ is eliminated as an answer.

### C. Where Do I Start?

**Answer:** 4

**Solution:**

Simplifying successively $\sqrt{13 + \sqrt{2} + \dfrac{7}{3 + \sqrt{2}}}$ first leads to

$$\sqrt{13 + \sqrt{2} + \frac{7(3 - \sqrt{2})}{(3 + \sqrt{2})(3 - \sqrt{2})}}, \text{ or } \sqrt{13 + \sqrt{2} + \frac{21 - 7\sqrt{2}}{7}}.$$

$$\sqrt{13 + \sqrt{2} + \frac{21 - 7\sqrt{2}}{7}} = \sqrt{13 + \sqrt{2} + 3 - \sqrt{2}}, \text{ or } \sqrt{16};$$

$$\sqrt{16} = 4.$$

### D. Prime-Time Viewing

**Answer:** $A = 6563$, $B = 83$, $C = 11$, $D = 5$

**Solution:**

This solution is found most easily by realizing that $D$ must be the smallest prime and then working backward to find the solution.

Case I:
$$D = 2$$
$$\sqrt{C - 2} + 2 = 2$$
$$\sqrt{C} - 2 = 0$$
$$C - 2 = 0$$
$$C = 2$$

Eliminate this answer, since $C$ and $D$ must be different.

Case II:
$$D = 3$$
$$\sqrt{C - 2} + 2 = 3$$
$$\sqrt{C} - 2 = 1$$
$$C - 2 = 1$$
$$C = 3$$

Eliminate this answer for the same reason as in Case I.

Case III:
$$D = 5$$
$$\sqrt{C - 2} + 2 = 5$$
$$\sqrt{C} - 2 = 3$$
$$C - 2 = 9$$
$$C = 11$$
$$\sqrt{B - 2} + 2 = 11$$
$$\sqrt{B - 2} = 9$$
$$B - 2 = 81$$
$$B = 83$$
$$\sqrt{A - 2} + 2 = 83$$
$$\sqrt{A - 2} = 81$$
$$A - 2 = 6561$$
$$A = 6563$$

Verifying that all are primes can be done by checking all primes less than $\sqrt{6563}$ or consulting prime-number charts.

### Problem Set 31
### QUADRATIC EQUATIONS

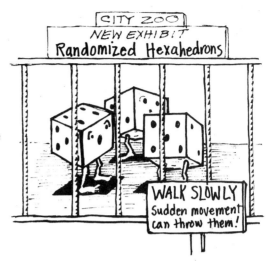

#### A. Randomized Hexahedrons

Stacey throws two dice. The difference in face value between the two dice is three, and the product of the numbers thrown is equal to twice the sum of the two numbers. *Show and solve* an algebraic equation that finds the numbers Stacey threw.

#### B. A Walk Through the Park

When Allen and Maggie reached retirement, they were finally able to buy the house of their dreams. It had a 40- by 72-ft rectangular yard. Maggie cultivated $\frac{5}{12}$ of the area in flowers, which she grew in an even border around the central court. Every morning Allen walked the dog around the central grass area inside the flowers. How many laps did he have to do to walk at least $\frac{1}{4}$ mi?

#### C. No Horsing Around

The Kentucky Derby is $1\frac{1}{4}$ mi long. If Surefire finishes second to Dud averaging 1.5 mph less than the faster horse and crossing the finish line 5 seconds later, does Dud break the Derby record of 1 minute, 58 seconds? Prove your answer.

### 31-A  RANDOMIZED HEXAHEDRONS

Stacey throws two dice. The difference in face value between the two dice is three, and the product of the numbers thrown is equal to twice the sum of the two numbers. *Show and solve* an algebraic equation that finds the numbers Stacey threw.

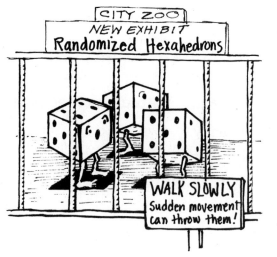

### 31-B  A WALK THROUGH THE PARK

When Allen and Maggie reached retirement, they were finally able to buy the house of their dreams. It had a 40- by 72-ft rectangular yard. Maggie cultivated $\frac{5}{12}$ of the area in flowers, which she grew in an even border around the central court. Every morning Allen walked the dog around the central grass area inside the flowers. How many laps did he have to do to walk at least $\frac{1}{4}$ mi?

## 31-C  NO HORSING AROUND

The Kentucky Derby is $1\frac{1}{4}$ mi long. If Surefire finishes second to Dud averaging 1.5 mph less than the faster horse and crossing the finish line 5 seconds later, does Dud break the Derby record of 1 minute, 58 seconds? Prove your answer.

## 31-D  EAT THE DUST

In a recent 10-km race, a runner finished 10 min behind the winner and ran at an average of 3 km/h less than the winner. What was the winner's average speed?

# Problem Set 31
## ANSWERS AND SOLUTIONS

### A. Randomized Hexahedrons

**Answer:** 3 and 6

**Solution:**

Let $x$ be the face value on die 1 and $x + 3$ be the face value on die 2.

$$\begin{aligned}
x(x+3) &= 2(2x+3) \\
x^2 + 3x &= 4x + 6 \\
x^2 - x - 6 &= 0 \\
(x-3)(x+2) &= 0 \\
x &= 3; \; x + 3 = 6
\end{aligned}$$

### B. A Walk Through the Park

**Answer:** $7\dfrac{1}{2}$ laps

**Solution:**

Let $x =$ width of border. The dimensions of the central court are $40 - 2x$ and $72 - 2x$. Since this area is $\dfrac{7}{12}$ of the original area, the equation $(40 - 2x)(72 - 2x) = \dfrac{7}{12}(40)(72)$ yields the border width.

$$\begin{aligned}
(40 - 2x)(72 - 2x) &= \frac{7}{\cancel{12}}(40)(\cancel{72}^{\,6}) \\
(20 - x)(36 - x) &= 7(10)6 \\
720 - 56x + x^2 &= 420 \\
x^2 - 56x + 300 &= 0 \\
(x - 6)(x - 50) &= 0 \\
x &= 6
\end{aligned}$$

The inside court has dimensions of 28 ft × 60 ft and a perimeter of 176 ft.

### C. No Horsing Around

**Answer:** No. Traveling at 37.5 mph, Dud takes 2 min to cover $1\dfrac{1}{4}$ mi.

**Solution:**

| | $D$ | $r$ | $t$ |
|---|---|---|---|
| Surefire | 1.25 | $x - 1.5$ | $\dfrac{1.25}{x - 1.5}$ |
| Dud | 1.25 | $x$ | $\dfrac{1.25}{x}$ |

$$t_{(SF)} = t_{(D)} + 5\text{ s}$$

$$\frac{1.25}{x - 1.5} = \frac{1.25}{x} + \frac{5}{3600}$$

Clearing of fractions yields

$$2x^2 - 3x - 2700 = 0$$

$$x = \frac{3 \pm \sqrt{21{,}609}}{4} = \frac{3 \pm 147}{4} = \frac{150}{4} \text{ or } \frac{-143}{4}$$

### D. Eat the Dust

**Answer:** 15 km/h

**Solution:**

Let $x =$ winner's speed and $x - 3 =$ runner's speed. Using $d = rt$, winner: $10 = x \cdot t$; runner: $10 = (x - 3)t_2$.

$$t_1 = t_2 - \frac{10}{60}$$

$$\frac{10}{x} = \frac{10}{x - 3} - \frac{1}{6}$$

Multiplying both sides by $6x(x - 3)$ gives

$$\begin{aligned}
60(x - 3) &= 60x - x(x - 3) \\
60x - 180 &= 60x - x^2 + 3x \\
x^2 - 3x - 180 &= 0 \\
(x - 15)(x + 12) &= 0 \\
x &= 15
\end{aligned}$$

**Problem Set 32**
*d = rt*

### A. Take a Hike

A hiker can average 2 mph uphill and 6 mph downhill. If the hiker goes up a hill and down and spends no time at the top, determine her average speed for an entire trip.

### B. Over Hill and Dale

Jeffrey visits his friend Kelly and then returns home by the same route. He always bikes at 6 mph when going uphill, 12 mph when going downhill, and 8 mph on level ground. Find the total distance he bikes if the total biking time is 6 hours.

### C. A Conductor's Nightmare

If it takes twice as long for a passenger train to pass a freight train after it first overtakes it as it takes the two trains to pass when going in the opposite directions, determine how many times faster the passenger train is than the freight train.

### 32-A  TAKE A HIKE

A hiker can average 2 mph uphill and 6 mph downhill. If the hiker goes up a hill and down and spends no time at the top, determine her average speed for an entire trip.

### 32-B  OVER HILL AND DALE

Jeffrey visits his friend Kelly and then returns home by the same route. He always bikes at 6 mph when going uphill, 12 mph when going downhill, and 8 mph on level ground. Find the total distance he bikes if the total biking time is 6 hours.

## 32-C A CONDUCTOR'S NIGHTMARE

If it takes twice as long for a passenger train to pass a freight train after it first overtakes it as it takes the two trains to pass when going in the opposite directions, determine how many times faster the passenger train is than the freight train.

## 32-D HIGHWAY PATROL

Howard travels on a busy highway having the same rate of traffic flow in each direction. Except for Howard, the traffic is moving at the legal speed of 80 km/h. In the same time that it takes Howard to pass a car going in the same direction as he is, 11 cars go by him in the opposite direction. By what percent is Howard exceeding the legal speed limit?

# Problem Set 32
# ANSWERS AND SOLUTIONS

## A. Take a Hike

**Answer:** 3 mph

**Solution:**

Since the distance is irrelevant, any distance that is a multiple of 2 and 6 will make the arithmetic easier.

|      | D  | r | t |
|------|----|---|---|
| Up   | 12 | 2 | 6 |
| Down | 12 | 6 | 2 |

The total time is 8 h, whereas the distance is 24 mi, yielding an average speed of 3 mph.

## B. Over Hill and Dale

**Answer:** 24 mi

**Solution:**

Let $x$ = distance uphill, $y$ = distance downhill, and $z$ = level distance.

$$\frac{x}{6} + \frac{y}{12} + \frac{z}{8} + \frac{x}{12} + \frac{y}{6} + \frac{z}{8} = 6$$

Multiplying both sides by 24 yields

$$4x + 2y + 3z + 2x + 4y + 3z = 144$$
$$6x + 6y + 6z = 144$$
$$x + y + z = 24$$

## C. Conductor's Nightmare

**Answer:** Three times

**Solution:**

Let $x$ = length of freight car
$y$ = length of passenger car
$s$ = speed of freight train
$zs$ = speed of passenger train

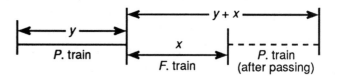

As the two trains pass when traveling in opposite directions, their relative speed is $s + zs$, or $s(1 + z)$. The distance traveled while passing is $x + y$. If $T$ is the time necessary for the passing process, from $r \cdot t = d$, $s(1 + z) \cdot T = x + y$. As the passenger train overtakes the freight train, their relative speed is $zs - s = s(z - 1)$. The time needed is now $2T$, while the distance is still $x + y$. The rate becomes $s(z - 1)2T = x + y$.

$$sT(1 + z) = 2sT(z - 1)$$
$$(1 + z) = 2z - 2$$
$$3 = z$$

## D. Highway Patrol

**Answer:** 20%

**Solution:**

Using the concept of relative speeds, the relative speed of two objects traveling towards one another is the sum of the two speeds, while the relative speed of two objects traveling in the same direction is the difference of the speeds. If Howard is traveling at $s$ kilometers per hour, $s + 80$ and $s - 80$ represent the relative speeds going in the opposite and the same direction, respectively. Letting 1 represent passing one car and using $d = rt$, $1 = t(s - 80)$ and $11 = t(s + 80)$. Since the time is the same, $\frac{1}{s - 80} = \frac{11}{s - 80}$.

Solving shows Howard's speed is 96 km/h, which is 20% more than the speed limit of 80 km/h.

**Problem Set 33**
**GRAPHING**

### A. Circumscribed or Inscribed

Find the difference in the areas between the figures formed when you graph $|x| + |y| = 4$ and $x^2 + y^2 = 16$ on the same set of axes.

### B. I See a Pattern

Find the rule of correspondence for the following table.

| 1 | 2 | 3 | 4 | 5 | ... $x$ |
|---|---|---|---|---|---|
| $\frac{1}{3}$ | $\frac{2}{5}$ | $\frac{3}{7}$ | $\frac{4}{9}$ | $\frac{5}{11}$ | ... $y$ |

### C. Double or Nothing

Consider the parabola $y = x^2 + x + 4$ and the three lines $y = 4x$, $y = -3x$, and $y = 2x + 6$. One of these lines is tangent to the parabola, one intersects the parabola in two points, and one does not intersect the parabola. Show algebraically which line is which.

### 33-A  CIRCUMSCRIBED OR INSCRIBED

Find the difference in the areas between the figures formed when you graph $|x| + |y| = 4$ and $x^2 + y^2 = 16$ on the same set of axes.

## 33-B  I SEE A PATTERN

Find the rule of correspondence for the following table.

$$\frac{1 \quad 2 \quad 3 \quad 4 \quad 5 \quad \ldots \quad x}{\dfrac{1}{3} \quad \dfrac{2}{5} \quad \dfrac{3}{7} \quad \dfrac{4}{9} \quad \dfrac{5}{11} \quad \ldots \quad y}$$

## 33-C  DOUBLE OR NOTHING

Consider the parabola $y = x^2 + x + 4$ and the three lines $y = 4x$, $y = -3x$, and $y = 2x + 6$. One of these lines is tangent to the parabola, one intersects the parabola in two points, and one does not intersect the parabola. Show algebraically which line is which.

### 33-D  WHO SET UP THIS MEETING?

An ant has traveled from (4, 8) to (4, 4) in 30 seconds. A mouse located at (–4, 2) traveling at 10 units/min wants to intercept the ant. At what point on the line $x = 4$ will the mouse intercept the ant?

# Problem Set 33
## ANSWERS AND SOLUTIONS

### A. Circumscribed or Inscribed

**Answer:** $16\pi - 32$

**Solution:**
The graph of $|x| + |y| = 4$ is a square with vertices $(4, 0)$, $(0,4)$, $(-4, 0)$, and $(0, -4)$, and $x^2 + y^2 = 16$ is a circle with radius of 4 and center at $(0, 0)$.

$$A_{(C)} - A_{(S)} = \pi r^2 - \frac{1}{2} d_1 \cdot d_2$$

$$= 16\pi - \frac{1}{2} \cdot 8 \cdot 8$$

$$= 16\pi - 32$$

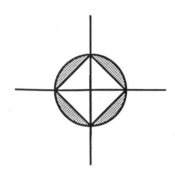

### B. I See a Pattern

**Answer:** $\dfrac{x}{2x + 1}$

**Solution:**
Examining the two sequences, the $x$ values represent consecutive integers, whereas the $y$ values are the set of odd integers greater than 1.

### C. Double or Nothing

**Answer:** $y = 4x$, 0 points; $y = -3x$, 1 point; $y = 2x + 6$, 2 points

**Solution:**
Solving the three systems simultaneously leads to the three equations $x^2 - 3x + 4 = 0$, $x^2 + 4x + 4 = 0$, and $x^2 - x = 0$. Using the discriminant gives values of $-3$, 0, and 9, respectively, leading to 0, 1, and 2 points of intersection, respectively.

### D. Who Set Up This Meeting?

**Answer:** $(4, -4)$

**Solution:**
The time for both the ant and the mouse to reach the point $(4, y)$ is the same. The mouse travels a distance of $\sqrt{(y + 2)^2 + 8^2}$, and the ant travels a distance of $y - 4$. The respective rates are 10 for the mouse and 8 for the ant.

$$\text{Mouse } t = \frac{\sqrt{(y + 2)^2 + 8^2}}{10}$$

$$\text{Ant } t = \frac{y - 4}{8}$$

$$\frac{|y - 4|}{8} = \frac{\sqrt{(y + 2)^2 + 8^2}}{10}$$

Simplifying this expression leads to the quadratic $9y^2 - 136y - 688 = 0$. Factoring as $(9y - 172)(y + 4) = 0$ yields $y = -4$ as the only logical solution.